WHAT KILLED JANE CREBA

WHAT KILLED JANE CREBA

RAP, RACE, AND THE INVENTION OF A GANG WAR

ANITA ARVAST

DUNDURN
TORONTO

Editor: Michael Melgaard
Design: Jennifer Gallinger
Cover design: Sarah Beaudin
Cover image: © iStock.com/Matteo Battagliarin
Printer: Webcom

Library and Archives Canada Cataloguing in Publication

Arvast, Anita, author
    What killed Jane Creba : rap, race, and the invention
of a gang war / Anita Arvast.

Includes bibliographical references.
Issued in print and electronic formats.
ISBN 978-1-4597-3506-4 (paperback).--ISBN 978-1-4597-3507-1 (pdf).--
ISBN 978-1-4597-3508-8 (epub)

    1. Creba, Jane, 1990-2005--Death and burial. 2. Victims of violent crimes--Ontario--Toronto. 3. Violent crimes--Ontario--Toronto. 4. Gangs--Ontario--Toronto. 5. Toronto (Ont.)--Race relations. I. Title.

HV6439.C32T67 2016   364.106'609713541   C2016-900878-9
                                                        C2016-900879-7

1   2   3   4   5   20   19   18   17   16

  **Canadä**

We acknowledge the support of the Canada Council for the Arts and the Ontario Arts Council for our publishing program. We also acknowledge the financial support of the Government of Canada through the Canada Book Fund and Livres Canada Books, and the Government of Ontario through the Ontario Book Publishing Tax Credit and the Ontario Media Development Corporation.

VISIT US AT
Dundurn.com | @dundurnpress | Facebook.com/dundurnpress | Pinterest.com/dundurnpress

Dundurn
3 Church Street, Suite 500
Toronto, Ontario, Canada
M5E 1M2

Dedicated to the artists who keep it real
so they can foster understanding and hope,
to all the families who have lost their children
at the hands of gun violence,
and to the advocates who are willing
to raise their voices.

Fighting crime by building more jails is like fighting cancer by building more cemeteries.
— Paul Kelly, author

Wish Canada still had the death sentence for the lot of them.
— Comment posted on a story about the Jane Creba murder trials

CONTENTS

AUTHOR'S NOTE

When I first began following the trials of the many young men charged with the killing of Jane Creba on the street outside of the Toronto Eaton Centre on Boxing Day 2005, I was disturbed by what was being reported in the news. Of course, we all wanted to blame the "thugs" — the young men whose parents had come from Jamaica — but the situation was far more complex than what was reported.

To arrive at the writing of this book, I spent years attending the trials, scouring academic journals and media reports, and conducting interviews, in addition to reviewing seventy-five banker boxes of trial files that one of the accused handed over to me. Those files form the bulk of the information I present in this book; they included police notes, wiretaps, forensics, statements of the accused, and statements from informants, in addition to thousands of transcripts from preliminary hearings and the actual trials. These files also included much information that I cannot write about for legal reasons.

Some of the people who were involved directly with this case believed I could add some substance, to tell their stories in a way that is not meant to garner sympathy or provide excuses, but rather, offer a level of understanding in a situation we should not be expected to understand, let alone accept.

The information I was given was not something anyone can easily get a hold of. Many people trusted me by giving numerous interviews. I gave them all the same promise — that I would share their truths.

I hope I have upheld that promise I made.

INDEX OF CHARACTERS DIRECTLY INVOLVED

TEAM A

Name	Aliases	Note	Association
Jorell Geraldo Simpson-Rowe	JoJay	Convicted of second-degree murder	Point Blank (Regent Park North)
Andre Thompson	Dre	Charged with manslaughter, later acquitted	None
Shaun Patrick Thompson	Speedy	Charged with manslaughter, later acquitted	None
(George) Vincent Davis	Visa	Charged with manslaughter, later acquitted	None
Unnamed young offender	White Chocolate/ Chocos	Charged with manslaughter, later acquitted	None

Name	Aliases	Note	Association
Louis Raphael Woodcock	Big Guy	Convicted of manslaughter	Former 5PG; none at the time of murder
Jevoy Karim Johnson	Jovi	Charged with manslaughter, later acquitted	None
Dorian Dayme Wallace	None	Dismissed, extradicted to UK, shot in chest	None
Tyshaun Barnett	Sido/Silo	Convicted of manslaughter	None
Kory Benoit-James	Kleezy	Informant	None
Andrew Smith	Optics	Charged with manslaughter, later acquitted	None

TEAM B

Name	Aliases	Note	Association
Milan Mijatovic	White Boy	Witness and victim, shot in leg	Silent Souljahs (Regent Park South)
Richard Steele	Richie/T	Witness (victim of robbery), charged with trafficking arms and cocaine	None
"Marz"(name is kept confidential for protection)	Marz Apocalypze/ Shurly	Charged with possession of drugs, key informant during trial	Brother in Silent Souljahs rap group
Eric Boateng	Boderick	Charged with firearms and drugs trafficking, killed in "call down"	None
Jermaine Osbourne	J9	Killed on streets	None
Anthony Moodie	None	Killed on streets	None
Jeremiah Valentine	Short/ Shackles	Pleaded guilty to second-degree murder (Jane Creba's shooter)	Silent Souljahs (Regent Park South)

INNOCENT VICTIMS

Name	Notes
Jane Creba	Murdered
David Audette	Shot twice in calf and ankle — neither shot penetrating skin
Jeyie Su	Two gun wounds, one in calf and one in ankle
Puo Yee Wiu (Helen)	Shot in left calf

OTHER ASSOCIATES

Name	AKA	Notes
Christoff Lewis	Creedy	Target in the Regent Park area, found guilty of murdering Kerlon Charles
Cleavon Springer	None	Key informant in Creedy's murder trial
Kerlon Charles	None	Shot dead in an apartment while trying to buy a gun, Creedy found guilty of the murder

INTRODUCTION

Question Marks

On December 26, 2005, guys with guns drew on each other on one of the busiest streets in Canada on one of the busiest shopping days of the year. The guys who drew the guns were almost all men of colour. The shots shook Toronto and the whole nation to its core as it took the life of a sweet, fifteen-year-old girl who was merely crossing the street in the midst of what all accounts would call a case of rival gangs taking their rivalries to the streets.

In the city that was known as "Toronto, the good," we had shit to deal with.

Jane Creba. Homicide #78/2005.

Just like that. A number.

She had a gentle smile. She was a grade 10 honours student and star athlete at Riverdale Collegiate. She lived a comfortably upscale life with her remarkably supportive family in Toronto's primarily Greek neighbourhood. Her home was just a stone's throw away from some of the major projects in Toronto, where guns were put on in much the same fashion most people would put on underwear. She was from a neighbourhood. They were from a hood.

Jane stole our hearts.

She was a beautiful child.

She was a beautiful child who shouldn't have died.

Like so many children.

Jane's shooting created terror, followed by demands that someone step up to prevent another such death. The Green Apple Project, named after Jane's favourite food, brought massive police raids to fourteen various low-income areas in Toronto, resulting in hundreds of detentions — primarily of young, black men.

The media had a heyday. Because selling news is sometimes about telling us to be afraid, we heard about gangs with guns gone mad. The media and police christened it "The Year of the Gun." Those reports were somewhat true. That year, nineteen people aged twenty-two or younger died at the hands of guns.[1] Those people wouldn't really make the news though.

Joan Howard lost her son to gun violence in 2003. She cried out against the contraband weapons coming up from the United States. She cried out against the shooting of her son, whose death elicited very little media coverage.

The *Toronto Star* reported at the time, "Howard says Prime Minister Stephen Harper's government is missing in action in making gun violence and its aftermath a national priority. 'I would never want to wish this kind of pain on anybody but maybe if it came to Harper's doorstep they would do something.'"[2]

Joan Howard is a black woman. Her son was a man of colour — a youth worker, a basketball coach — shot in the head at his apartment building while on his bicycle.

Two years later, in 2005, the coverage changed. Gun violence became the news.

Jane Creba's death forced us to pay attention. That attention was focused on the incident itself, as opposed to the underlying causes ... but that's what most of us who open a newspaper, turn on the news, view our tweets, or check out the latest on our computers want. We want digestible pieces. Instead of being encouraged to dig deeper, we want to be "in the know." The media would deliver what we wanted. That message was easy: be scared of every young, black guy living in projects in Toronto because they were all part of gangs. Crips or Bloods. They fell short of using the N-word, because that would be politically incorrect. So we just heard this: rival gangs.

On the tenth anniversary of Jane's death in 2015, the *Toronto Star* published an article about how right the police got it.[3] The article cited police as being content that they set a precedent — four men in total were convicted for her death (two for murder and two for manslaughter), but only one bullet hit Jane, and only one man fired the bullet that killed her. The *Toronto Star* called it "The Jane Creba Effect" — four convictions for one bullet. And one of the men charged never even fired a gun. They were all black. We were told they were all "thugs."

They were allegedly all part of gangs.

You got time for a story?

The media did.

The N-word is a highly politicized term that some people have said ought never be pronounced. Political correctness doesn't change perspectives, it only changes the ways people can express prejudice. People always find new ways to say it. It might not be *boy* and it might not be the N-word.

It might be a far more clandestine and infinitely more dangerous disguise. Just like the cover of this book.

What colour did you assume that person's skin was?

It's only natural. We've been taught these assumptions.

Thug is a word usually applied only to bullies and they are presented in typical ways — in hoodies and in high-tops with a bit of bling around the neck and usually with some variation of brown skin.

But there are thugs who are icons in corporate culture. Like Steve Jobs. A celebrated entrepreneurial thug. Thugs are academics who claim that their version of bullying is "academic freedom." Like Phillipe Rushton, who sought to maintain a stereotype that penis sizes, race, and intelligence were all related. Thugs are police who claim that their bullying is "keeping people safe" even while they break the law. Thugs are members of our governments who claim that their bullying is "in the public interest according to their election mandate" as they monger fear and create new legislation to deal with the fear they've mongered. Thugs can be the media reporters who sometimes hound people to get stories. Inside their own realms, the bullies don't get called thugs. Sometimes they don't even get called bullies. They get called *successful*.

Bullies are everywhere; they hide behind their own rhetoric to justify their behaviour.

Most bullies don't unpack their own behaviour. They take their baggage and sell it to their corporate boards, to the pulpits, to the classrooms, to Parliament, to the public. What we think is a thug isn't white and well off. We think that the street is the only place you can find thugs.

We'd like to believe we don't have racism in Canada. We were, after all, the final destination of the Underground Railroad not that long ago. We represented the North Star and the road to freedom.

We don't have twenty-one-year-old white-supremacist Dylann Roof walking into a Charleston church Bible study and slaying nine people of colour. And then going to prison where he was raped and tortured. We don't have cops shooting down black guys like they do down in the U.S. We don't have the fifty-year-old man shot eight times in the back after running away from police for fear that he would be jailed for failing to pay child support. He'd been pulled over for a burned-out tail light. What was his name, again? Walter Scott. His family will remember, but we likely won't. The blame was laid on that one cop who set Walter up, planting a taser beside Scott as he was dying — all that captured by someone walking by who happened to have a cellphone. We don't have the hundreds of other incidents that don't get captured on a cellphone.

We don't have Freddie Gray, who had his spine fractured as he was being brought into custody, and we don't have the protests of Baltimore. Even if the cops who caused his fatal spinal injuries have been indicted and that bit of unrest settled, we aren't done with unrest. For every moment captured by a camera, scores more go unseen. Unrest goes quiet. But it's there. It's here.

It's far easier to lay blame on individuals rather than systems. Blame those cops who abuse their power. Blame the thugs who commit crimes. Maybe make the prison deal with all this blame. Make it out all black and white, or all light and dark. Black is wrong. White is right. Light is joyful. Dark is scary. Let's forget about anything remotely in-between.

In Canada, we don't have Freddie or Walter. We didn't have Rodney King. We didn't have Malcolm X. We didn't have Martin Luther King. Because we don't have riots and blatant issues of racial profiling and police brutality, we'd like to think we don't have those issues. Of course, we *did* have racism when the Underground Railroad brought too many ex-slaves to the East Coast and they all got put in a place called Africville, an area the city of Halifax neglected to the point of squalor. And, of course, we *did* have racism when the Japanese were interned during the Second World War and had all of their belongings taken from them. And, of course, we *did* have racism in the residential schools and our treatment of First Nations people. And we still have racism now in the hushed sentiments of "those Muslims," and the attacks on mosques and spiteful acts carried out against women wearing hijabs.

But no. We like to think we don't have racism like in the U.S. We don't have potential presidents saying that we should ban all people of a particular faith from coming to our country.

What we have is systemic … something we disguise.

On December 15, 2014, some nine years after the Creba killing, the *Toronto Star* broke a story that the Toronto Police Service had finally brought in a psychologist from the U.S. to investigate racial profiling by members of the police force. So now we have proof that there are problems. They range from police racial biases to the carding of individuals based on race to the detention of young, African-Canadian men even when they are not being investigated in a criminal case. These practices lead to feelings, perceptions, and behaviours that run deep and cause insecurity and even hatred. It's been there a long time, but at least we are finally talking about it.

The practice of carding had been long-standing in Toronto. It's a simple process of a police officer stopping, questioning, and putting the name of anyone who looks questionable into a database for further reference — no matter what the person was doing. In a city of roughly two hundred thousand African Canadians, there were over one million carding incidents in a two-year period. As shown in the "carding database," there was an egregious over-representation of young black men.

A *Toronto Life* journalist wrote of being carded seven times for doing nothing more than being black in public. Desmond Cole had the nerve to write about "The Skin I'm In." Toronto got a new African-Canadian chief of police who said that he had been carded as a teenager for wearing a ball-cap backwards. He justified the policy by saying that he somehow deserved it; he shouldn't have dressed that way. There was a polite controversy going on in Toronto. That's how we do things in Canada. Politely. It's why people like to visit here. It's why people like to live here.

We also have laws we follow to ensure we remain polite.

Carding is clearly a violation of the Ontario Human Rights Code and the Canadian Charter of Rights and Freedom. This was confirmed by various studies that indicted not only the police, but many legal administration and enforcement agencies.[4] In 2015, the new Liberal government of Canada decided they would deal with this. No more carding. No more racism. Easier said than done. This was going to be a long fight. You can't just tell cops to stop racist practices because the government has made it illegal. It will go underground and sideways until conversations between the affected communities and the police take place. These conversations take years, maybe decades. Until they do, both communities will continue to feel threatened.

There remains a great deal of insecurity around race, profiling, and the relationships between police, the community, and the journalists who have to report what is going on. Most of us don't ever need to think about it. It doesn't concern us.

Unless you have a child who is caught in the crossfire. Or unless your kid keeps getting asked what he's doing because he has the wrong skin colour and was maybe driving the wrong car or walking in the wrong neighbourhood.

Nobody ever expects that a few minutes of someone else acting out on their insecurity will take a life. We think we will grow old and die of natural causes. We live our lives accordingly. Take speed seriously on highways. Don't engage in dangerous activities. Wear a bike helmet. Wear sunscreen. Cross the street on a green light. Teach our children to be kind and expect kindness to be returned. Well. That's most of us. We're not children expecting to die. We're not expecting the worst when we venture out on the streets. We dress each day to go about our business — yoga pants for the gym, a suit for work. In most cities in North America and Europe, we don't expect violence to erupt. We think, if we keep living our routines and being good citizens, the problems of the world won't affect us.

Grief doesn't end overnight, and racism doesn't end because we pretend it isn't there. And a city awash with gunplay doesn't get fixed by police forces that take away basic rights for the select people of colour who just happen to live in impoverished neighbourhoods. We don't fix things when we have overcrowded jails and treat people as guilty before proven innocent. We don't fix things when people think defence lawyers are about "getting people off," rather than participating in a system where evidence must be examined and laws must be followed.

Very few of us know what it's like to spend a night in the hole of a detention centre like the old Don Jail, where feces backed up regularly from sewers into the cells, rats became pets, and two of the three guys in the cell built for one were sleeping on the floor. Yet many of us say "they deserve that" or that "they shouldn't be credited for their time in detention." We don't know what a "call down" is. That will be explained later. It ain't pretty.

If we could shake those perceptions for a little while, if we could walk a mile in those high-tops, we might get closer to being done with racism, and the violence it leads to.

Millions of dollars were spent on the Green Apple Project. Hundreds of police were assigned to the surveillance. Twenty-five men were arrested in a massive raid in June 2006. Fifty-six men with direct or indirect relation to Jane's death were arrested in total that year. Almost all of them were African Canadians.

Nine young black men and one "wannabe black" young offender were charged with her murder. The wannabe never made it to trial because they figured out he didn't actually have a gun. The other white guy who was directly involved that day (and probably had a gun) was never charged. Instead, he became a witness. The majority of men were acquitted because there was no evidence they participated in anything other than being present that day. But many of those eventually acquitted spent four years in jail awaiting trial anyway. The guys who waited in jail were one colour.

Only one bullet struck and killed Jane.

Only one man killed her, and he eventually told the courts that he did it. The cops were never sure which bullet actually killed her. So his admission was key.

One bullet. But four young African-Canadian men were convicted of murder by a prosecution that changed its story at each trial, despite stern warnings from the judge that this wasn't the way to do justice. These kids definitely had problems and they may have been guilty of a lot of things. But murder?

"Who killed Jane Creba?" is an easy question to answer. It was Jeremiah (Short) Valentine and his .357 Magnum. It was young men with guns from the ghettos. Thugs, as the press made them out to be.

What killed Jane is a way tougher question to answer.

The trials may be done, but the bigger question marks remain.

1

T-dot-O

Rap it everywhere I go.
— Kardinal Offishall, "The Anthem"

Yonge Street. The longest street in Canada. *The Guinness Book of World Records* recognized it as the longest street in the world until 1999. It starts at Lake Ontario in Toronto before wending its way north through suburbs and, eventually, into the forests and rocky scrapes of Canada's near north. There, it somehow transforms from Yonge Street into Highway 11, connecting the hubbub of Toronto with the moose of Algonquin Park and the endless frontier of the Canadian Shield, where there are vast skies and virtual emptiness. Most Canadians don't live the solitude that is the "North," and which is what most people outside of our country think of when they picture Canada — polar bears, moose, trees, ice, and rocks. But we're more urban than people think.

Toronto is only about a two-and-a-half-hour drive from the U.S. border. North of Toronto, Canadians own rifles to shoot moose and bears. Close to the border, where most of our population lives, our kids get contraband handguns from the neighbours to the south, who have much laxer gun laws.

Toronto. T.O.,we call it. T-dot-O.

The Zanzibar strip club on Yonge Street is lit up with neon — flashing orange and red signs a hundred feet tall stand over its meagre entrance, trying to seduce people to come inside. It's probably the place table dancing in Canada originated, and lap dances are cheaply served up by women in spandex ranging in ages and nationalities. Neon is everywhere on Yonge — the open signs at the money exchanges and hole-in-the-wall nail salons and places that offer to unlock your phone. The two-hundred-foot signs that advertise new television shows bounce their reflections off the glass highrises. Everything flashes for attention.

Voices rebound off the pavement and sidewalks — some, the homeless asking for change; some, the outrages of a dispute; some, brazen teens singing in a drunken stupor; most just the idle conversations of people walking to and from the points in their lives. There is a constant white noise of cars travelling, of taxis honking, of subways rumbling underfoot. And about every ten minutes, the sound of a siren echoes as it takes an emergency patient to one of the many hospitals in the downtown core.

Most people don't bother to pick out the nuances of conversation and noise and light until they are told they need to pay attention. On the day after Christmas 2005, we were told in no uncertain terms.

The cops and newspapers had already decided 2005 was the Year of the Gun in Toronto. There had been way too many gun homicides that year — the heat from the concrete jungles was seeping out into the polished neighbourhoods of the suburbs and the traditional safe zones of the middle class. Gang warfare was out of control. The town was no longer "Toronto the safe," or "Toronto the Good," or "Toronto the big city where shit doesn't happen like it happens in L.A."

That year there were 70 homicides in the city, 78 potential ones investigated. The year before there had been 60.

In the grand scheme of things, Toronto's murder rate wasn't that high. From 1998 to 2007, the homicide rate was 1.8 per 1,000 people. Put in context, Winnipeg's was 3.2 and Edmonton's 2.9.[1] Was the city as big and bad as L.A.? Not so much. Their rate was 10 per 1,000. Philadelphia was a whopping 23, and even the quiet retirement city of Phoenix, Arizona was 13.1.[2] Go figure. That's where many middle-class Toronto snowbirds go to escape winter.

But 2005 still got called the Year of the Gun in Toronto, because of those 70 homicides that year, 52 were by gun, almost double the 27 in 2004.[3] And the kicker was the death of Jane Creba the day after Christmas.

December 26 is a holiday in Canada called Boxing Day. It's a big shopping day with great deals — people picking up boxes of new stuff. The stores were packed with people as usual that day. And the big Eaton Centre shopping mecca on Toronto's Yonge Street was, as per its tradition, busting out onto the sidewalks and streets. As dusk approached, pedestrians ruled the roads by the mall; Christmas lights brought the windows to life with their train sets running, glittering gowns flowing, and mechanical elves dancing and making gifts, while the usual neon light continued to flash.

To the east of this shopping hub is a low-income housing neighbourhood called Regent Park. A concrete labyrinth for displaced immigrants and the generally impoverished — almost seventy acres in total, with people just crammed on top of each other. Seventy acres of cells, mostly three-storey, run-down apartments where the inmates could get out if they could only find work that would raise them out of the dependence on socially assisted housing. The average income in Regent Park at the time was half of what the average Torontonian made; 68 percent of residents were considered to live below the poverty line, and there was a significantly higher population of people under the age of eighteen than anywhere else in Toronto. As the U.S. had discovered in cities like Detroit, New York, and L.A., when you cram that many poor people together in that big a space, there are bound to be issues.

Marz was in the Regent Park project housing on Boxing Day. A young man of Jamaican descent who had seen his share of heat in the hood.

The party was on at Elmer's. Elmer was a nine-to-fiver who Marz had known since infancy. Their buildings were next door to each other. Elmer's place was a home, as opposed to a hangout — it spoke of the working class, with its mismatched furniture and old appliances. The home had the standard pictures of kids on the fridge alongside their artwork from younger years.

Elmer picked up trash — like junk, scrap metal, and steel — and sold it. Elmer's mom and pops weren't really involved with the hood politics. They said hi to the neighbours and made small talk. That's about it. It's what a lot of people in the hood do. Stay low, keep your family close and your nose out of trouble. Embrace your ancestry and your children.

Short and Boy were at Elmer's, too. Drinking beer. Shooting the breeze. They weren't the types who stayed low and out of trouble.

Growing up, Short was called Too Short because of his small stature. He got over that in his teens when he managed to get over the 5′8″ marker and condense his moniker. Marz didn't think of Short as a particularly good-looking guy. According to him, Short was … well … short … and had "kind of buggy eyes," and wore his hair "short-cropped … like it was just growing back from a haircut or something." Short was also heavily scarred — on the forehead, between the eyes, and on each arm. His police files never identified the scars, but clearly he had a history of confrontations.

Boy was different. First of all, he was white, so he was sometimes called White Boy. With his formal name as Milan Mijatovic, he certainly didn't fit the stereotype of the Jamaican Canadians that the majority of people in the city just assumed were the problem people in Regent Park. But that's the way assumptions and stereotypes work. A way to simplify what's actually complex.

Boy was about the same height as Short and he was good friends with Marz's youngest brother, Kareem. He even gave Marz's mom bail money to get Kareem out of detention one time. The money came from drugs and guns, but that's just what friends do for each other. Boy didn't typically get into much trouble even though he was known to be a major dealer. It was debatable whether or not he packed a weapon. He had Short do that for him on Boxing Day, even if Marz would eventually say otherwise: "I would assume [Milan/Boy] had a gun," Marz eventually told police when pushed to testify. Marz's brother wound up getting a gun for his own protection when he dealt. "And my brother's not hardcore into it, but considering that those were his friends, and people are gunning at him, he got his gun."

At Elmer's, Boy and Short came up with the idea that they should go down to the Eaton Centre to get some shoes for their kids. Marz thought it best not to go downtown that day. He was the wisest of the lot. As he eventually told the court: "Cause I wasn't in the mood to be in any situation where anything can happen. Where I'll be involved in that situation.... Boy really wanted to go down to get the shoes. I forewarned him. Like situations might pop off down there. You might see people you might not like."

What was going on in the hood? Well, there was trouble between some groups of people. Some guys from north Regent Park weren't getting along with some guys from south Regent Park. Bigger than that, though. Some guys from various areas of Toronto weren't getting along with other guys in various areas of Toronto. Not gangs. Individuals. Guys who just didn't like each other.

There was too much already going on in the hood. Lots of shout outs and shootouts. The guys who'd been around for a while, like Marz, knew better than to put themselves out there on a public day when all this shit is going on. Boxing Day. Caribana. Big festivals and gatherings were a no-no if you knew people were looking for trouble or looking for you. Why bother putting yourself out there on a day when you know all your enemies are going to be out? Marz was several years older than those other guys heading downtown; he'd developed a code that comes with maturity — you don't go looking for shit on busy days, let alone take your problems to the streets.

Inability to see the logic of this code might have something to do with the fact that adolescent minds aren't fully developed. Laurence Steinberg is a professor of psychology at Temple University in the U.S. who has written extensively about the neuroscience of risky behaviour in youth. His brain imaging studies have shown that teenagers, for instance, respond to peer pressure in ways that make them behave recklessly. Neuroscientists at the Belmont hospital in Massachusetts have shown that adolescents rely much more on a part of the brain called the *amygdala*, while adults rely on the more developed frontal cortex.

What does this mean? It means teenagers brains aren't yet wired quite right to make sound judgments. It means they use the "reactive" part of the brain more than the "thinking and strategizing" part. Of course, it doesn't mean teenagers are wired to carry guns. But if they are, chances are they aren't modulating emotional responses the same way that adults do — they aren't thinking about the consequences. Seems the mood swings, temper tantrums, and stupid, risky behaviour exhibited in teens doesn't have so much to do with raging hormones as it does with a brain that isn't yet "working" as adults understand. Throw in some other stupid teenagers who aren't logically wired, and the risk-taking ramps up considerably.

All this came together in Regent Park that day, with the more mature guys knowing rivalries needed to stay in the hood, while the younger punks wanted to head out into the world, rivalries be damned. As Marz would eventually tell it, "you can't fix stupid" — even though he likely wasn't referring to neuroscience. Bottom line is that most kids are going to rely on their peers to tell them what's real rather than listen to the older folks passing on their wisdom.

Like many teens, they thought their parents or anybody even a little older didn't understand the world they lived in — and certainly didn't have advice to give them.

Like many teens, they got stuff wrong.

And so it was. As the party at Elmer's wound down, Marz was adamant that he wouldn't be putting himself out there, even if Boy was one of his brother's closest friends. Marz opted to go home to watch some daytime drama on the television, while Short and Boy headed to Yonge Street. The two had already been targeted in their neighbourhood. Shot at several times, they wouldn't take public transit and knew better than to stand on a street corner trying to flag a cab. They called one instead.

Marz didn't know it at the time, but one of the reasons Short had been targeted was because he was ratting out some other brothers in an area of western Toronto called Black Creek. There was also a housing project north-east of Black Creek nicknamed "the Jungle" — high-density, socially assisted housing not unlike Regent Park. Short had lived there at one point, but now he was just serving as an informant to the cops about some of the guys living there and in Black Creek. So, it was ironic that on this Boxing Day, Short was wearing a T-shirt with a big stop sign on it. All the rage with some of the "tough guys" from the States. Under the big red stop sign was a single word. Snitching.

Seems Short was okay to don the wear without walking the talk.

2

Short, Big Guy, JoJay:
AKA's, Thugs, and Hoods

I was born and raised in the ghetto.
Until it's my time to come.
When it goes down and die young.
With the good ones they call us thugs and
  hoodlums.
… I'm from a park where we don't play.
                    — Point Blank, "From a Park
                          Where We Don't Play"

In 2005, Regent Park was one of the oldest of the social housing projects in Toronto and one of the city's biggest problem
areas. It was essentially divided into a north and south side,
with rivalries separated by just one street that cut east–west
through the middle of it — Dundas. Short, Boy, and Marz
lived on the south side. Marz lived there with his two brothers and mom. One brother was finding his way in the world,
and one was finding his way on the streets — that was Short
and Boy's friend, Kareem. Kareem had a record and a pro-
pensity for hanging with the wrong boys, but he got lucky on

Boxing Day; he would have gone downtown with Short and Boy if he weren't locked up in the Don Jail, detained on drug and weapon charges. As Marz told it "85 to 90 percent chance [his brother] would've been with them."

Kareem was a member of a rap group called the Silent Souljahs. They were from the south side of Regent. Point Blank was a rap group from the north side. Some guys actually didn't give a shit what side of the park you lived in because everyone was suffering the same. But some guys did. This is what the media told as the main story in the aftermath of the shooting: north against south.

Two gangs. Too easy. Two rap groups with some rivalries and some members and affiliates who carried guns — Marz's brother carried a gun, Short carried a gun, and likely Boy carried one. But they weren't two gangs. These were groups of poets who had affiliations with other poets trying to get out of a ghetto through their music. Being a hip-hop artist required artistry — an ability to play with words and ideas. Almost all of the guys there on Boxing Day had tried to play with poetry at some point. Had tried to rap. Who would ever think that poetry could cause rivalries? But it did.

In 2005, Short was living in Regent Park. But he had grown up in an area northwest of downtown called Jane and Finch. It's an area of social housing most notorious for being the riskiest place in Toronto for a child to grow up. Innocent people had been killed walking down the street or just hanging out with friends. Jordan Manners, a fifteen-year-old boy who lived and went to school there, was the first person to be shot inside a high school in Toronto. William Appiah was just hanging out on a basketball court when he was shot down. Parents often didn't know if their kids would make it home, or whether their kids were into the gang and drug scene or not. If their boys *had* been pulled to the periphery of the thug life by the glitter of gangs and money, chances were a lot higher that they wouldn't see them turn into men.

Directly south of Jane-Finch, on the other side of the 401, is the Black Creek area. At one point as a young adolescent in junior high (grades 7–9 in those days), Short had also lived in the projects there. It is a pretty big area stretching from Jane and Lawrence down to Keele and Rogers, and as far east as Dufferin. A particularly heavy area for low-income housing was a street called Martha Eaton Way (originally a set of high-profile condominiums for professionals, but now worn down, slummish apartment buildings), but since that area was short on amenities, most of the Black Creek boys gravitated to Dufferin and Eglinton for action, and sometimes crossed into the territory of Jane-Finch or headed south into the downtown core.

Here's the thing about hoods and gangs. They are more liquid than solid. Mostly, they are make-believe. We might have a map that roughly shows where crime is pronounced. But it's really only a map showing where socially assisted housing exists.

Most of the people who live in these hoods are hard-working folks just trying to get food on the table and keep the hydro on while working a minimum-wage job — sometimes two. They've escaped some hardships, but not all.

These main hoods in Toronto are home to a substantial number of recent immigrants. Of course, that's an aspect of systemic discrimination and segregation (no longer mandated, but still a reality) that is difficult to address. How do poor people get into housing and out of these "ghettos" that thugs try to reign? That's a mighty big hole to climb out of.

There have been lots of efforts to "fix" the problems in all of these areas. Sometimes that means community groups working with police. In extreme cases, it means efforts to gentrify.

In 2014, the University of Toronto released a report on the demolition and resurrection of Regent Park, citing it as an ideal opportunity for "Social Cohesion in a Contested Space," which is the title of the report. It states:

> Regent Park is Canada's oldest and largest social housing project and is currently undergoing a fifteen to twenty year revitalization process. Since the 1940s and 1950s, when Regent Park was first redeveloped from "slum" to social housing project, the neighbourhood garnered a stigmatized reputation for high rates of crime, poor social conditions, and physically isolating infrastructure. In 2005, Toronto Community Housing Corporation (TCH) initiated a process of redevelopment in partnership with private developer Daniels Corporation to transform the neighbourhood into a mixed-tenure, mixed-income community. Regent Park will no longer consist entirely of social housing units, instead, the residential make-up will be roughly 70% market rate units and 30% social housing units once the redevelopment is finished. The physical transformation of the neighbourhood is

> happening alongside coordinated efforts to
> facilitate the social integration of new and old
> residents to ensure a cohesive environment
> for all Regent Park residents.[1]

It's all well and good for planners and academics to discuss the future of the area, but in 2005, Regent Park was 100 percent socially assisted housing with a considerable reputation. It wasn't all bad, and there were a lot of efforts to promote a positive sense of community. But none of the efforts were on the scale of the plan that eventually would come into place and yet solve only *some* of the problems while simultaneously displacing many people who relied on socially assisted housing to keep a roof over their heads. And people who actually called this home, and called their neighbours their friends.

In north Regent Park, Point Blank rapped that they came "from a park where we don't play."

In south Regent Park, the Silent Souljahs were rapping about "working it out."

Most of the OG's (original gangsters) knew rap was about the systems they were fighting rather than the individual rivalries or people in various neighbourhoods. The older guys also had respect for authority, parents, and family. And they respected what police called the G-code. It was a code that Short wasn't following. It was a code that Marz and Boy would eventually be expected to break.

What's the G-code? Unwritten rules about taking care of your people, especially if you lived in one of these hoods. The G-code isn't really "gang code," as the police and media describe it; it's an understanding amidst a group of minoritized people who fear authority because of their own bad experiences — particularly with racial profiling — but still respect police authority as a necessity in dangerous areas and times. And the G-code is like any code of brotherhood — whether it's police brotherhood, army brotherhood, or biker brotherhood.

One of the unwritten rules revolves around snitching; it's a big no-no. That works fine when the G-code is taking care of you, but if you're suddenly facing trouble, it might be easier to talk to the cops than end up serving time. But snitching leads to a lot of heat in the hoods. Something Short knew about as a target for his own snitching. And he wasn't the only one breaking the G-code.

One of the guys being snitched on was Christoff "Creedy" Lewis from Regent Park. Seems some of the thugs didn't have a problem pointing the finger at him for whatever reason. Less heat? A sense of justice? Not sure.

Creedy was the fellow who led another man named Kerlon Charles to a vacant apartment in a building quite a ways from Regent Park. Kerlon thought he was going there to buy a gun; Creedy knew otherwise. Kerlon was beaten with pool cues, then one of the six or so attackers took a TEC-9 semi-automatic and shot Kerlon eleven times in the head and torso as he lay face down on the floor. It was one of the first homicides in Toronto in 2005. A cold, calculated kill.

It was a while before Creedy got tied to that case and convicted of second-degree murder. Before the police made that connection some five years after Kerlon's death, Creedy had shot a guy named J9 seven times in the back. He eventually got charged for that as well. J9 was Jermaine Osbourne, allegedly present at the Boxing Day shooting of Jane and shot just a couple of weeks before the big raids would come down in relation to the Creba case. His family celebrated his twentieth birthday in the hospital with J9's brand new baby girl. But J9 wasn't celebrating. He was in a coma and died just six days later. He never made it to trial for the Boxing Day events.

Before that all happened, Creedy was doing some introducing of guys in Regent Park. Guys who could sell drugs. It seems Marz's brother met Short through Creedy. Creedy was a kingpin in the Regent Park area. He was the reason there were shootouts in the many years leading up to the Year of the Gun. Marz called Creedy "the original victim" up in the upper echelons of the Silent Souljahs rap group because he would "big them up" by playing their music when he DJed in the clubs (as opposed to playing the music of Point Blank). He was likely the key reason any rivalries had started, simply because he didn't play the music of another rap group from Regent. Creedy called himself a "Blood." Whatever that meant.

Marz's brother was a rapper with the Silent Souljahs. But Marz didn't see himself as belonging to any "side."

Hard to play it neutral as it turned out, and 2005 was definitely a year when you couldn't just sit on the fence. Seems Marz picked his side the day he was seen outside wearing a Silent Souljahs T-shirt in the fall. A couple of the Point Blanks didn't like that.

"What the fuck you wearing that for?"

"It's just my brother's group. I support everyone."

As he would tell the court during the preliminary hearing, "In 2005, you (couldn't) be in between. There is no neutral ground." Rivalries were clearly heating up between the two groups of music makers.

On October 28, 2005, Marz was going to go to a movie with his girlfriend. As they crossed the street to get in a cab, two guys in masks on bikes fired shots on Marz as he scrambled to safety. He was pretty sure it was members of another rap group affiliated with Point Blank, who at the time went by the name TnT (based on their names Turk and Tyke).[2] TnT — who later became TnT Sick Thugz — were later attached to another shooting at the Toronto Eaton Centre in 2012. They sang about violence and Marz reported that they actually perpetrated it targeting individuals in the south part of Regent Park. When Point Blank stopped rapping in about 2013, TnT/Sick Thugz had replaced them in the media and on police radar as the "Sic Thugs Gang."[3]

As for Marz, no gang affiliation. He just wanted out of the neighbourhood. His girlfriend wanted him out. But sometimes you just don't have a choice about where you live.

Just three days after the shooting by Marz's cab, on Hallowe'en night, a gunfight erupted behind Marz's building with at least thirty guys involved. It's a miracle nobody died. Another shootout happened in Regent Park in mid-November. Marz reported that this was the work of the rival TnT and Silent Souljahs.

Creedy was apparently one of their main targets. They didn't get him in the mid-November shootout in Regent Park, or on the day when a car he was sitting in got riveted with bullets. After those incidents, he went into what Marz called "hyper-paranoid mode" — changing his cellphone every few days, never staying in the same location for more than a few days, and certainly keeping on the down low in public.

No way Creedy would be out on Boxing Day. Marz was right. Too much popping off in the "park where we don't play."

But it wasn't as easy as just those rivalries between Silent Souljahs, Point Blank, and TnT. It was more about personal rivalries and allegiance to friends; issues less threatening to the public than gangs and far too nuanced to explain.

There are bad boys in every neighbourhood, it's just that some neighbourhoods have conditions that tend to produce more. Short was one on the bad boys. He had a lengthy criminal record for drugs, assaults, break-and-enters, and drug trafficking. He wasn't a gang member. He was an entrepreneur, who ran up against some other entrepreneurs in the drug trade.

He had a lot of enemies, especially from Black Creek, and at one point even told police that word on the street was that there was fifty thousand dollars up for grabs for his head. It's nice to feel important.

Boy had enemies from both Black Creek and Jane-Finch. Same place Short had enemies.

A lot of dealers in the suburbs don't have enough customers in their own area, so they sometimes migrate downtown to deal. And that was crossing territories. Whether you're a record store owner, a mom-and-pop restaurant, or a drug dealer, nobody wants competition coming into their turf.

Boy and Short also had enemies called the Po Boys (or Project Originals), who named themselves this because the Atkinson Housing Co-op where they resided (with boundaries Dundas West to the north, Queen to the south, and Bathurst and Spadina on either side) was the first (i.e., original) public housing conversion in Canada. They started off just promoting community pride, but eventually those ideals fell to the wayside and the Po Boys, like many of the young men, turned to the drug trade. The Po Boys claimed strong allegiance to the Bloods. Their rivals included people from Regent Park and the Jane-Finch corridor, even though the Regent boys *also* referred to themselves as "Bloods through and through." Go figure.

It seems that the L.A. gang culture didn't really transplant so well to Toronto. Too many boys confused about what it meant and where the intersections spelled a territory. Some of them still wore the colours — red for Bloods, blue for Crips. But honestly, very few were actually associated with either L.A. gang.

Some reports claimed the reason for the Boxing Day shootout was because of a rivalry between a kid named JoJay (a Point Blank affiliate because his uncle was a member of the group) and Boy (a Silent Souljahs affiliate). Not so easy. Not so true. Another of the reported rivalries was between Short and a guy in Black Creek named Big Guy. That wasn't quite true either.

Big Guy wasn't a part of any gang. The police and media used these guys' nicknames to imply they were all gang members, but the truth was much more simple than that. Fact is, all of them got their handles when they were children. It's a standard part of Jamaican culture. Big Guy wasn't called Big Guy because he was a significant menace; he got that name for his stocky physique as a boy.

Did Big Guy have friends? Yes, he did. But they weren't gang members either. The usual concept of a gang is a group of individuals who commit crimes together. The truth is that most "gangs" have much more considerably fluid membership. So-and-so is friends with this other guy, so they hang out. Sometimes friendships go awry and those bonds break. Street gangs don't have initiation rights or oaths or even anything remotely resembling a commitment. They're often just groups of teenagers who come together — usually to protect each other from bullying or threats of violence. Bullying and threats are all too common in difficult neighbourhoods. Why wouldn't a person want to ensure they had the protection of friends?

Still, Big Guy had a reputation with the police as a previous associate of the Weston Road and Lawrence Avenue 5 Point Generalz (or 5PGz), who were based out of an area just west of Black Creek. He had an extensive rap sheet for guns, drugs, resisting arrest, and assaults (including on officers). The truth is that he spent most of his time in the Black Creek area working part-time at a community centre, helping young children. His police files don't mention the community work, or his coaching of baseball teams in his neighbourhood, or his regular church attendance.

Despite what was in his police file, he wasn't actually associated with the 5PGz. Yes, he knew them. But it wasn't friendly. There was apparently another Black Creek gang called the Gatorz who weren't too friendly with the Five Point Generalz. Big Guy wasn't a part of that gang either.

It seems the police files had a lot of wrong information about Big Guy.

While Big Guy lived with his parents, he also paid a bit of rent to another guy in the Black Creek area — a guy named Kory Benoit Jones. Kory's crib was a basement apartment in a house. His mom didn't care for his lifestyle and kicked Kory out at a young age. When he had money for the bus, he sometimes made it to school. But mostly he just sat around his apartment smoking dope. School is hard when you're virtually illiterate. Welfare carried him some of the time, but to keep up with his pot habit he would do break-and-enters and deal in crack and pot.

It was tough to make his rent, so he tried getting a couple of roommates. That's how Big Guy ended up there in the fall of 2005. Kory would smoke pot every day all day, and Big Guy just used the place once in a while to bang a girl or hang. Kory didn't have much use for Big Guy. And at the end of the day, Big Guy had zero use for Kory. Kory was just a little guy in his mind.

Big Guy saw Kory as something of a wimp. Kory didn't much care because he was stoned most of the time and had become completely complacent about anything going on in his apartment.

Those tensions aside, Kory's apartment was pretty useful for anyone who was trying to stash arms or anything else remotely illegal. He had a "smoking room" — really just a dingy room not much bigger than a closet — where he and anyone hanging at his crib could go smoke. The ceiling in the room wasn't finished, just beams and fibreglass insulation. It was a perfect spot for guys to hide any guns they were carrying or trying to sell, and Kory would always play the stupid, stoned guy who knew nothing about this.

Big Guy stashed his 9-millimetre there.

Big Guy was also friends with a young offender named Jorell Simpson Rowe, whom he met at school. He went by the nickname of JoJay because it just rolled off the tongue a lot easier. JoJay had a difficult past. When JoJay was young, his father was deported, leaving the boy to be raised by an often violently abusive, alcoholic mother. He struggled in school because he had a number of learning disabilities that would not be discovered until well after the Boxing Day shooting.

Ironically, his brother would be quite successful, even going to York University on a football scholarship. Such would never be the case for JoJay.

Big Guy, JoJay, Short, Boy, J9.

All these guys were just guys who hung out with their friends. They hailed from all over the city, many with their friendships dating back to childhood. Some of these guys had crossed paths before, but most had not. They were just all there on Boxing Day.

3

Hip Hop. Out!

Dear Hip Hop, I'll love you 'til I dic
To taste the grace of your embrace, I will try
My mission is to utilize my skills on the mic
To rid you of the losers, abusers and stereotypes
— Dan-e-o, "Dear Hip Hop"

So, how to escape the hood and its poverty?

Well, you can try to get out through sports — what middle-class white kid doesn't want to escape mediocrity in a suburban cul de sac (i.e., dead end) to become a hockey star, and what impoverished black kid doesn't want to play for the NBA? Not much of a chance any kid is going to the NBA or the NHL. You can dream though.

You can try to get out through education. But if you struggle with learning disabilities (especially undiagnosed), or aren't academically inclined, or aren't adequately supported by various resources available to people with higher incomes, chances are against you.

There's another way kids think they can get out of the projects — making it big in music. It's not easy; not many kids get signed to record labels, but you can dream. You can dream of doing just what hip-hop artists like Dan-e-o do, utilize skills on the mic to deal with the abuses and stereotypes.

Or you can just try to deal with the pain of poverty. That might be either by getting high or helping others to get high and hoping that you don't die doing either. If you aren't athletically or academically inclined, the latter two options are where you might land. Hoping to make it out through fame or some version of fortune — both defined by street cred. Because, let's face it, nobody wants to be stuck making minimum wage.

But rapping it out isn't the same as gangsta rapping it out.

Silent Souljahs and Point Blank were rap groups from Regent Park. Not even gangsta rap groups, and a far cry from gangs. TnT? They were a little different in terms of what they rapped.

There are significant differences in the music scene with respect to rap and hip hop. Those types of music aren't the same. Rap is an actual genre of music, while hip hop is a subculture that is formed of the trivium of rap, dance, and art. Gangsta rap is a subgenre of rap that promotes crime, misogyny, murder and, ironically, racism.

Gangsta rap is seen by many as synonymous with hip hop — all of this music gets thrown into one big category that ignores the many nuances. The fact is, hip hop is a genuine art form born out of poetry and celebrating stories through numerous plays on language. At its best, it does what any art should — it invites us to wonder, to play, to think about meaning in layers and labyrinths. And because it is strongly affiliated with breakdancing and graffiti art (not to be confused with graffiti vandalism and community tagging), it does what visual art and dance do. It invites us to look at our culture. And to find beauty even where there is tragedy.

Amidst the mundane and profane. Find the sublime.

Remember that the creation of art is what makes us human. And most art comes out of a struggle. Art comes out of a desire to be free. That could take the form of cave dwellers facing unknown beasts, Mozart playing games with the aristocrats, or Picasso questioning realists. Pretty much any place you find art, you find struggle lifted up by imagination. Hip hop was born of people's desire to defy the odds that were stacked against them by their race and poverty.

Clive Campbell is seen as the originator of hip-hop music. He moved from Jamaica to the Bronx in the late sixties and began DJing with two turntables and a system set up to play loud bass. His impressive size gave him the nickname Hercules, shortened to Herc, and eventually, Kool Herc. DJing a party in 1973 in the rec room of an apartment building with a few hundred people, he discovered that breakdancing became particularly pronounced during the breaks of songs — the parts of a record where there was only instrumental. He figured out that by using the two turntables to extend the musical breaks, the dance crowd went crazy. From that rose the MC, the Master of Ceremonies. The MC was the rapper who added poetry to the breaks.

In his book *Can't Stop Won't Stop: A History of the Hip-Hop Generation,* Jeff Chang identifies the roots of hip hop in the social policies of "urban renewal" mixed with "benign neglect." The building of New York's Cross Bronx Expressway ravaged many of the city's ethnic neighbourhoods, destroying homes and jobs and displacing poor black and Hispanic communities to areas like the South Bronx. The government turned a blind eye to those affected; the youth needed a way to express their own culture.

So the music was born out of this displacement as a means for people to tell their stories through rhyme (rap) and empower themselves through the four elements of hip hop: DJing, MCing, graffiti, and breakdancing. The narratives of the time were positive, creating value out of races and places that previously only seemed to be realms of social devastation.

The rivalries between MCs were healthy competitions that originated in wanting to out-do each other, first at block parties, but eventually, as the popularity of the music grew, at larger venues and clubs.

Flash forty years forward and true hip hop continues to provide messages of faith, hope, inclusion, creativity, and transformation. Hip-hop artists tend to put down the sub-genre of gangsta rap, which rose in the eighties and nineties and proved to be lucrative, with rappers like Ice-T and NWA getting gold records. Gangsta rap involves the celebration of violence — definitely not part of the original hip-hop message. It essentially promotes killing, misogyny, profanity, rape, drug-dealing, and gangs, as it ironically also delivers an essential message of inherent racism — i.e., "Kill your brothers." "A to the motherfuckin' K." Use an assault rifle to do it.

Spike Lee, in his film *Bamboozled*, sums up the way that many hip-hop artists feel about gangsta rappers. He draws an analogy between gangsta rap and blackface performances in which performers were made to look African American and acted in stereotypical ways. Neither form promotes a positive image, and they both ultimately enhance racialized depictions.

When hip-hop artists speak the truth, they *do* speak of discrimination, of police brutality, of the realities of poverty, addiction, and violence, but they do so in a way to condemn current institutions that create and sustain these harsh realities, not condone violence and treating women as trash. Quit the hatin' and the stuntin'.

True hip-hop artists raise questions. For instance, why, in 2016, are academics still writing about the misrepresentation in the media of young black men, particularly those associated with crimes? There are numerous studies every year that conclude that young, black males, when they appear in the media, face exaggerated negative associations, limited positive associations, and a distortion of problems as well as missing stories and histories. When we see young, black men in the media, we tend to see their mug shots. The black men don't appear as people, but as images without a history. In deep contrast, serial rapist and murderer Paul Bernardo was depicted in the media at his wedding; Luka Magnotta, the psychopath who dismembered his lover and sent parts of him to various government officials, was frequently shown in photos taken for a fashion magazine. And the kid who shot up a bunch of people gathered at a church, Dylan Roof. He was shown only as some freak of nature neo-Nazi white guy by his mug shot.

The white men committing crimes are the freaks. We hear their stories, we hear about their lives. The black men are the stereotype, and we don't hear about their histories.

Out of this, we get some genuine art rising up to challenge the systems. Use the mic to rid the stereotype.

But gangsta rap would have us believe that the mainstream media has it right. "Black men are violent." So it's a significant fight for those artists who want to break that image, or at least talk about it.

Dan-e-o spoke about violence in an interview for a documentary produced about Regent Park artists. As far as violence in hip hop is concerned, he wants artists to be cognizant of the stereotypes they may be promoting. "I think honestly, it just comes from a history of struggle. A history of hardship. And I think that can come from anywhere. Just like violence can come from anywhere, violence and music can come from anywhere." He recognizes that images and examples of violence are common place in hip-hop music, but adds, "I think that we have to do our best — when you're using these images and concepts that involve violence — speak out against it because it's not what we want. I don't think that's what anybody wants."

The violence is only one aspect of rap and hip hop that many find offensive. Misogyny runs rampant in some rap, with lyrics like "ninety-nine problems but a bitch ain't one" or the videos that show women only as subservient sex toys for men.

The rap artists who belittle women in their lyrics are pretty much doing the same thing the gangsta rappers are doing: put down someone else to make yourself feel important. Start fights with your brothers instead of attacking the systems. Treat the women like dirt instead of recognizing they are your mothers and sisters and caretakers, not just "hoes" for you to walk on the same way society walked on you.

Now some female hip-hop artists are out there combating those images and sending positive messages. Michie Mee, who grew up the Jane-Finch hood, raps of empowerment for young women. Such artists work to ultimately deliver messages of hope, not of hatred.

Hatred doesn't grow out of an abyss, unless we call that abyss "ignorance." It grows out of misunderstanding and an inability to empathize. Psychopaths like Paul Bernardo, Jeffrey Dahmer, and Adolph Hitler couldn't empathize because they just weren't wired to do so. But imagine if every one of us who *is* actually wired right empathized with various points of view. How rich would we be as a society?

Music doesn't grow out of an abyss. It grows out of a culture and an effort to engage in conversations that will elicit empathy. Sometimes that culture is surrounded by hatred and misunderstanding. Some fools who rap certain kinds of music continue to breed that hatred themselves. So some voices will reach us and garner empathy and other voices will only serve to reinforce stereotypes.

The Silent Souljahs and the Point Blank groups were called gangs instead of artists. But most of their messages weren't of violence. Point Blank's video about being born in the ghetto focused on caring for young boys who were lost when their brothers were either dead or in prison. Silent Souljahs's video about working it out sought to give people hope. And yet, both groups were depicted as gangs in the media.

One point of confusion with the media was the group TnT (Turk and Tyke), younger associates of Point Blank. They were arguably advancing the gangsta agenda. But TnT/Sick Thugz came to rule the north side of Regent Park only after the Creba killing, after Point Blank and Silent Souljahs dissolved. In TnT's 2009 video "TnT Is Nice," they show a drive-by shooting in which a friend is killed, then specifically make mention of D-boys (the common term for drug dealers) and south side (Regent Park) boys as not being welcome to their hood. The video opens with a warning of explicit content, and indeed, the whole video is about threats and revenge through gunfire.

As one confidential informant said after the Creba shooting, "Some guys just do the rhymes. What these guys rap about is real. They don't just talk it. They do it." They rap their own wannabe rap sheets.

If they were actually working with the true slang of rap, they would be more accurate saying TnT is wack. But maybe irony was their point. Their lyrics were quite the opposite of Silent Souljahs' concept of "working it out."

If there were rivalries between Silent Souljahs and Point Blank/TnT, they were easy to understand because of the challenges facing artists in Toronto. According to most hip-hop artists in Canada, the scene is very difficult to break into, so when a DJ was playing one group and not another (as Creedy had been doing), that tension might heat up. The club scene was where rap groups needed to become known and it would be a diss to be ignored in favour of someone else from the same hood. To get played on radio, you can't just be an urban start-up any more. Only those with financial backing will get played. Where does that backing come from? Well, mostly it's artist grants that happen on federal, provincial, and some local levels. But there are committees that decide who gets that grant money and who doesn't. So often it's about who you already know and who knows you.

That wasn't always the case. When a Toronto hip-hop radio station was, after many years of battling for a spot on the FM frequency, finally started in 2001, urban artists finally had a place for their voice. Flow FM played many up-and-coming hip-hop artists; those who self-recorded at last had a place to be heard. Flow FM was the starting point to getting their own record contracts with the larger institutions, primarily in the United States, which had the population eager for rap.

Silent Soljahs may have been getting played up in the clubs, but they certainly didn't have a record contract. Neither did Point Blank. And in 2005, TnT was just affiliated with Point Blank.

Rival interests were indeed alive and well. They were a factor in the events leading up to the Boxing Day shooting. But to say that it was two gangs duking it out on Boxing Day, as the Crown and the media presented it, confuses the relationships.

Art and violence are never so simple.

Often, art tries to reflect the complexity of relationships. But that complexity may be lost in efforts to bring evidence to court and then to report.

Where there isn't freedom (i.e., respect and love), violence will necessarily seep into the cracks of an ideology and expand to fill up the space. Racism often creates those cracks where violence can find its roots. And then the violence erupts in those cracks and spreads out into hatred. It's not a thing we can kill with pesticides of any sort. Not bullets. Not jails.

Artists will continue to try to explain the complexities of life's challenges — whether they be personal or social or political — through words, visuals, and music.

Big Guy's dad is from Jamaica. He's a poet, an artist, an iron worker, a father. His poet (spoken word) name is Rapper. He's seen everything during his life; enough to know to remain soft spoken. He knows everyone in his neighbourhood and they greet him with respect. He has endured the stereotypes that suggest black youth don't have fathers, and he has written and spoken about the reasons for that. Systemic racism.

Big Guy was raised with respect for his people. The family brought their faith from Jamaica and they worked to maintain it in their new land. They were regular chuchgoers, and participated in church events. Rastafarianism is a religion and way of life originating in Jamaica celebrating divinity, resistance, and pride in African heritage and it can be found co-existing with Christianity in many churches.

Bob Marley, a devoted Rastafarian who combined his music with a spiritual sense of Jamaican culture and identity, popularized the term Buffalo Soldiers. What he tried to address in his music was a struggle of the black man. He likened the Buffalo Soldier — the black U.S. cavalry regiments — to those who "fight for survival."

The Buffalo Soldiers were also referenced by a Toronto hip-hop artist named K'naan in his song "Wavin' Flag." Before these artists, Buffalo Soldiers were just black troops who had fought against the Aboriginal population in the U.S. to help the (white) foreigners settle. Apparently, it was the Aboriginal people who nicknamed these men Buffalo Soldiers, because of their tenacity (and possibly hair texture).

When K'naan's song hit the charts, very few people would know there was a reference point of Toronto and this artist's own "fight for survival" and his own "redemption song" — a struggle towards an emancipation from mental slavery that was also deeply rooted in Marley's beliefs. Rise up. Just like a wavin' flag.

Few artists in the Toronto hip-hop community could ever reach the status of K'naan. He was born in Somalia in

1978, and came to Toronto after many a civil war broke out in his homeland. He was a refugee who grew up in some of the very hoods at the very same time as people who were involved in the Jane Creba murder.

Back in his homeland, he witnessed people killed blatantly. In Toronto he had friends murdered, commit suicide, and be deported back to countries where they would face death. In one interview, K'naan said that the violence he witnessed in Toronto actually rivalled what he had seen in his homeland.

These Somali refugee boys faced having their basic rights to security, education, and respect largely neglected. Because they were black and lived in a brand-new ghetto that was only about six buildings in an area of Toronto known as Jamestown (an area of Rexdale), they regularly faced various forms of harassment. K'naan's mother's home was often raided by police. K'naan didn't take this well. In interviews, he eventually spoke about rising up against the police and striking them with his fists despite them holding guns to his head. He admits to being the first one in a fight and the one who carried a gun by his waist. He admitted to going to jail and having a brother who has been in jail virtually his whole life in Canada.

Despite having served time in jail as a gun-slinging thug, in 1999 he presented a spoken word piece to the United Nations High Commissioner for Refugees in which he criticized the United Nations for its failure to support refugees during the Somalian civil war. In 2001, he toured the world. In 2005, the year of Jane's death, he produced his debut album, *The Dusty Foot Philosopher*, and won the Juno Award for Rap Recording of the Year (the Canadian equivalent of a Grammy), a coveted Polaris prize, and even won an MTV music video award.

The Jamestown area of Rexdale, notorious for thug activity when K'naan was growing up, was just the same as any of the other hoods — Regent, Black Creek, Jane and Finch. What he sang about, what eventually became a Coca-Cola anthem for the 2010 FIFA World Cup Soccer, was actually about growing up poor, disrespected, a person of colour struggling not to just survive, but to be "emancipated from mental slavery" — just as Bob Marley had sung about. But his reference point wasn't Jamaica. It was Somalia. And it was Toronto.

People rapping in the hoods of Toronto could only dream of becoming an international sensation like K'naan. People like Big Guy and JoJay kept rapping and hoping. Silent Souljahs and Point Blank were just trying to break into the local scene. Forget about the dream of the international, mainstream market.

K'naan's story is just the story of one man coming out on top from the projects in Toronto. There is a way out. And it has to be poetic. But sometimes that poetry gets lost in hopelessness, and the hopeless just need the feeling to band together.

What is a gang really? An organized group of criminals? The guys there on Boxing Day were hardly organized. They were banded together by music, but the music had lost its way. Music needs money to record, to buy gear, and a McJob didn't beat selling drugs on the streets for getting cash. And the biggest money to be made in the drug trade was in selling crack.

The crack dealers clearly hadn't read *Freakonomics*, the book by University of Chicago economist Steven Levitt and

New York Times journalist Stephen J. Dubner. The book discusses the poor economics of crack dealing:

> A crack gang works pretty much like the standard capitalist enterprise: you have to be near the top of the pyramid to make a big wage. Notwithstanding the leadership's rhetoric about the family nature of the business, the gang's wages are about as skewed as wages in corporate America. A foot soldier had plenty in common with a McDonald's burger flipper or a Wal-Mart shelf stocker. In fact, most … foot soldiers also held minimum-wage jobs in the legitimate sector to supplement their skimpy illicit earnings. The leader of another crack gang once [said] that he could easily afford to pay his foot soldiers more, but it wouldn't be prudent. "You got all these niggers below you who want your job, you dig?" he said. "So, you know, you try to take care of them, but you know, you also have to show them you the boss. You always have to get yours first, or else you really ain't no leader. If you start taking losses, they see you as weak and shit."[1]

Not Buffalo Soldiers. Foot soldiers.

Now these guys in Toronto weren't nearly as organized as a crack gang. Sure enough they bought that stuff from guys who wouldn't be touched on the street. Fact is that any kind of orchestration will distance the players from the actors. These guys were all pretty much footmen and single entrepreneurs with a fluid level of governance where some guy would help them get the stuff and then they would just head to the streets. Levels of leadership were transient. And even if they hadn't read *Freakenomics*, they pretty much knew from their neighbourhoods and the experiences of their friends that they had a one-in-four chance of being killed. There weren't crack gang rivalries, like some sort of corporate structure here. It wasn't like BlackBerrys versus iPhones. It was just guys who didn't fully understand, as Levitt and Dubner showed, that a crack dealer actually has a higher chance of death than an inmate in Texas on death row.

You deal shit, you're gonna make enemies. You make enemies, you might go down.

Now a lot of the young people there that day had been essentially raised as Christians who could relate to the redemption songs of both the Rasta (and Coptic Christians) and the Baptist Christians. All of the boys there that day were brought up to believe in God, and to believe in resistance. Some of them had not been taught to believe in themselves. Others had not.

Still, they had dreams and had to believe there was a way out of suffering.

"To rid you of the losers, abusers, and stereotypes."

4

R-E-S-P-E-C-T

"Sock it to me ... sock it to me ... sock it to me."
— Aretha Franklin, "Respect"

Life on the streets is tough enough for a guy, try being a girl there. Girls have to deal with the boys declaring undying love, knocking them up, and then moving on. They have to deal with disrespect voiced in the music of the gangsta rappers. They have to deal with all the discrimination women in general face, and the additional challenges of being a person of colour and locked into the cycle of poverty. Sometimes just as "baby mamas" when their men have left them pregnant, moved on, and can't or won't contribute to caring for the children. Another family stuck on some form of social assistance.

The young men at the Boxing Day shooting were connected to women with their own sets of rivalries. Phone taps of the suspects under surveillance picked up conversations with women who made references to carrying knives and threatening other girls for hooking up with men they thought were their boyfriends. The girls were in trouble with the law for this sort of activity, but it just wasn't as important as what the boys were up to. A few times the women mentioned that the men were going to help "rough up" their rivals; but clearly these young women didn't really know how low they really ranked.

No guy was ever going to go rough up another girl over some petty jealousy; too much heat for no gain. The girls should have been paying more attention to some of the nastier rap music on the streets that referenced women as "bitches" and "hos" — that normalized the objectification of women, justified their exploitation and even victimization, and, in some instances, glorified prostitution and pimping. Not a lot of respect in those lyrics.

A young woman named Patricia knew street life all too well. And she knew where women ranked in it.

She was born in Jamaica and moved to Canada at age five. She went to church every Sunday with her parents, but home life didn't quite jive with the peace and love they spoke and sang about in church. Life wasn't easy with an alcoholic father who would beat the children and then say he loved them. The concept of right versus wrong wasn't exactly clear under his supervision, and yet, somehow, weirdly enough, Patricia loved her dad.

Patricia's mom knew it was best to stay out of the way when dad was acting up. She kept to her nursing job and tried to raise the kids. Despite the challenges on the home front, Patricia did well in school and was an honours student when she turned twelve. Stuff changed quickly though. She was raped by a family friend (which she was terrified about disclosing), and then sent to a foster home for reasons she would never know.

It was in foster care that she first learned how bad some kids can be. Her home life had always been very strict

— school, homework, chores, and church — but at the foster home, she watched kids her age get away with a lot. It was here that she was introduced to street life. It started innocently enough. Smoking cigarettes, then pot. Staying out late with the wrong kinds of kids. That stuff happens to a lot of teenagers, but the foster home was ripe for picking up a bad attitude.

When she went back to her parents a couple of years later, she didn't have much use for strict regulations on her behaviour, religious obligations, and curfews. She became more defiant, more rebellious, and more interested in being on the street than in the shackles of home life. At around the age of fifteen, she was introduced to cocaine, which came with welcome pain relief, and the less welcome addiction.

A lot is a blur during this period. When an addiction takes over, all sense of right and wrong goes out the window. She would hang out with guys who could take care of her addiction. Typically, they weren't the churchgoers her parents had been. When these guys didn't like her attitude, they'd beat her down, and then apologize and tell her how much they loved her. It actually wasn't that different from the home environment where the concept of love was forged. Some cycles are pretty rough to kick.

So her teen years were spent largely in and out of trouble, but mostly in it. Then she fell in love — or what a confused teenager might think is love — with a dealer. At nineteen, she gave birth to Tyshaun. His dad was in and out of her life — mostly out — and coke was still very much on the scene. She got pregnant with Sasha a couple of years later and gave up the cocaine during that pregnancy. But times were tough for the single mother who was white-knuckling her way with the addiction. Patricia's mom was the one who came to her rescue when she couldn't cope anymore and needed help with the kids.

In the days before video surveillance, shoplifting was how Patricia made ends meet. She was quite adept at it. She could lift just about anything that had resale value on the street. She knew it was wrong to bring the kids to the stores when she did it, but she had no choice; they needed the money. At a young age, Tyshaun even told her he wouldn't go into a store when she was stealing. "It ain't right, Mommy," Patricia recalled him telling her. She brought the kids anyway; she knew that if she got picked up by the cops, her mom would show up and take them. If she left the kids at home, she couldn't be sure that anyone would know they needed care.

The streets were too hard on her. In and out of prison. On and off drugs. When things got really overwhelming on the streets — after a few too many beatings by a boyfriend or a rough time on the coke — she'd commit a crime just to try to go to jail for a break. And when things got really bad, she heard that an easy way to off oneself is a shot of coke to the arm. Thankfully, she missed the vein. And there were those way-too-many-other times she would tell her kids she'd soon be home, but then get arrested or beaten up and not show up for them. Or show up after a beating. Or show up on coke. And watch her kids cry.

She knew she couldn't hack it as a single mom in her condition, but she didn't know where to turn. The Children's Aid Society was sometimes there for Patricia, giving her a place to live, but sometimes their rules didn't make sense. On one occasion they provided her with a motel room to stay in, but then one social worker came and said it wasn't a safe place for the kids, so off Tyshaun and Sasha went again to a foster home, leaving Patricia alone in a rundown room with little hope for a way out. She knew from her own personal experience that a foster home wouldn't give her children the guidance they needed. But she felt utterly helpless.

She would get her kids back for periods of time. Meanwhile, her son was struggling in school and was diagnosed with ADHD (all the rage for diagnoses in the late nineties) and put on a low dosage of Ritalin. He was put in a special education class with five other kids and four teachers. Patricia was at a loss. She barely knew how to take care of a child, let alone one with special needs.

When she consulted another specialist, Patricia was told that Tyshaun didn't have ADHD, but just needed to be kept busy — that she needed to pay more attention to him as he was acting out because he wanted love. He wanted parenting. Patricia took him off the Ritalin and the Children's Aid worker said she wasn't providing for his basic needs.

Off they went to a foster home again.

Patricia didn't know it, but she certainly wasn't alone in her plight. In the Toronto area, black children were placed into foster care and group homes at a substantially higher rate than white children. Even years later, the practice is still commonplace. According to the *Toronto Star*:

> Numbers obtained by the *Star* indicate that 41 per cent of the children and youth in the care of the Children's Aid Society of Toronto are black. Yet only 8.2 per cent of Toronto's population under the age of 18 is black. By contrast, 37 per cent of kids in the care of the

Toronto CAS are white, at a time when more than half of the city's population under the age of 18 is white.[1]

Another pandemic for the racialized and impoverished that doesn't get the attention needed for people to learn that solutions are necessary. As Valerie Steele, president of the Jamaican Diaspora Canada Foundation, said, "we believe ... there's been too much silence and not enough activism, not enough holding certain entities accountable for what is happening." Many other leaders specifically cited the number of children in foster care, sparking a fear that they are being isolated and harmed in the same way Aboriginal children were in residential schools. They are children getting lost.

When Tyshaun was fourteen, his dad came back on the scene. Tyshaun and Sasha were supposed to go to live with him. Here's how that went.

Dad wasn't really there for them either. He was in and out of jail, but when he was out he was busy with shady deals (mostly drug dealing) and running a restaurant/booze can with his mother, Tyshaun's grandmother. Tyshaun's dad just handed the kids over to his own parents, who had way too many of Tyshaun's cousins already living there because their parents didn't have the means to care for them. Tyshaun and Sasha's dad showed up often with money for them, but not much in the way of love and support. The two kids slept on the floor. And, in their young minds, they felt that nobody gave a shit about them.

After stints of rehab, Patricia made an effort to turn her life around. She took Sasha with her when she moved north of the city, but Tyshaun was already finding his way in street life, and certainly didn't want to move out of Toronto with his mom. He alternated instead between staying at his grandma's, living in a room above the restaurant, or staying with friends. Some cycles are just tough to beat.

Patricia was surviving as a dancer at a strip club. Clean, but still hooked up with a guy who wouldn't hesitate to beat her if he didn't like something she did, or said, or didn't do, or whatever his mood was. The final crash was yet to come. One night while dancing at a club named Misty's in an industrial area in Barrie, a city an hour north of Toronto, Patricia got harassed by a group of men from a nearby armed forces base. She ignored them, and apparently one of the men didn't appreciate that. He continued to be derogatory and aggressive, but eventually left.

Once the shift was over, one of the other dancers asked Patricia if she could drive her home to the army base where she lived. The problematic guys were nowhere around, and it was on her way back to her boyfriend's house in Wasaga Beach, about an hour away, so she agreed. They hopped into Patricia's boyfriend's truck and made the twenty-minute drive to the base. After dropping off the other dancer, Patricia made a stop at a public washroom on her way home. When she came out, the man who had been harassing her at the club was waiting for her. Did the other dancer set her up? Why did she stop at a public washroom instead of using the washroom of her colleague? Hard to say.

He tried to drag her into a nearby wooded area, but Patricia had watched *Oprah* and learned from the show that the one thing you fight against is being moved to a secluded spot. So she fought tooth and nail. Since he wasn't going to win, he strapped his hands around her neck and choked her, leaving her for dead.

But she wasn't dead. She eventually got up and tried desperately to call for help as her throat closed in, her clothing covered in urine and feces — the typical release of a body dying. She struggled back to her boyfriend's truck and managed to drive to the nearby town of Angus. She was honking at vehicles passing her; nobody stopped. She managed to find a military police vehicle in town and they got her to the hospital. Ironically, all that was going through her head at the time was that her boyfriend was going to beat her if she didn't get his truck back.

Patricia spent a full two days in the hospital with doctors telling her they couldn't believe she survived. Photos were taken, showing the choke marks, the swelling around her neck, the cuts and bruises to her face and body. She was asked to identify the attacker, remembering only the way he walked and the shape of his head. Through some miracle, perhaps because he already was known to be a problem in the military, the police tracked him down. His name? Michael Shellington.

Shellington was charged with aggravated assault — not attempted murder. When Patricia asked why he wasn't being charged with the more serious offence, she was told it was because she was black. Because she was a woman. Because she was a stripper. Because she had a criminal record.

It was a full year before the preliminary hearing took place, and at it, Patricia's character was raked over the coals by the defence lawyer. For the first time ever, Patricia had a full appreciation of why a rape victim would never want to go through the court system. But she fought through it with stern determination. This was a man who'd tried to kill her because he deemed her a piece-of-trash stripper. Somehow, she held on to her pride.

Shellington pleaded guilty before the trial started. He received a mere eighteen months. At least he was kicked out of the army.

But there was a piece of Patricia that wanted to see him found guilty in court instead of getting away with a guilty plea that protected his identity. She wanted to see him suffer. To see his name made public. She wanted to see something that might make up for the sheer terror she felt whenever darkness came that she knew she would have to live with every night for the rest of her life.

No media ever reported the life-threatening assault or the name of the man responsible.

For a long time Patricia had wanted out of the life she had fallen into. Just like her son and his friends. Out of poverty mostly. But also away from the men who treated her the way the misogynistic rap lyrics suggested women should be treated. Always a strong woman, she wanted to be stronger, loved, and respected. She would eventually find that, just as her son would eventually find his path. But they had a ways to go.

5

Crack 101:
Make Sure You Have Friends

I used to keep a grudge on me.
I can't deny I still do
Just being truthful.
Wondering could I be fruitful too
The lifespan of a brotha ... it ain't getting no higher
Negative thoughts corrupt our minds with man-
made desires
I walk my path in solitude cuz no one understands
the intricate instructions to raise a young black man
— Silent Souljahs, "Work it Out"

Tyshaun didn't need to know what his mother was going through because he was going through his own trials and tribulations in Toronto. It wasn't easy for a sensitive kid who always felt people were laughing at him because he had "special needs," but somehow he gained the respect of the streets, and never let them know that, deep inside, he was still a scared and shy little boy.

It's pretty tough to grow up with a mom who was an addict and a dad who was too busy running an afterhours booze can on top of running various scams and dealing drugs to be around his son. Tyshaun was okay with his mom doing coke at home, because then he could take care of her. But when she was in jail, he felt lonely and frightened.

At school, he was embarrassed and ashamed of being in a special education class, so instead of going out and making friends, he stayed at home and watched television. And so, by the age of seven, he felt alone. He had no mom. He had no dad. He had special needs. He didn't feel like he had friends.

When his mom got really bad into the coke, Tyshaun went to live with his grandma. But Patricia's mom was a busy nurse; she was older and didn't really understand how kids desperately want to fit in. All the other kids at school had cool lunches and clothing — when other kids had Snackables, he had apples; while they had cool clothing and the latest shoes, he had no-name knock-offs. Kids can be pretty tough on other kids they don't see fitting in. It was another reason Tyshaun pretty much kept to himself. He was an embarrassed little boy.

When he started middle school, he was still enrolled in the Catholic school board and regularly attended church with his grandma. But the special bus that he took to school made him wonder what the other kids would be saying about him. The fact that he had a bit of a lisp didn't help.

Years later he would say, "I don't know if they ever called me stupid. But I had it in my head that that's what everyone thought of me."

He went to live with his dad's parents at the start of high school. That house was a far cry away from the strict, religious home of his other grandparents. It housed a minimum of thirteen kids at any time. The top floor was the "favourite kids," who had their own bedrooms. The middle floor was where the girls stayed, and the basement was where all the boys went, all sleeping on a bunch of mattresses on the floor. And because this grandma owned the restaurant and booze can with Tyshaun's dad, she would leave the house at 7:00 a.m. and be home around 3:00 a.m. At this time, one of his cousins gave him the nickname Silo (sometimes Sydo or Sido). That was just what happened in the culture: nicknames. Not gang names. Just terms of endearment.

So this was where Tyshaun grew up — a place awash with kids out of control.

Tyshaun's dad was friends with Lawrence Woodcock (the spoken word poet known as Rapper), who had a son named Ralph, aka Big Guy. Big Guy and Tyshaun hit it off and hung together a lot even as very young children.

By the time he hit his early teens Tyshaun's older cousins introduced him to the profits of selling weed. In grade 9, he was dealing on his own, smoking the weed he didn't sell. Petty theft, intimidation, and mugging became the norm to make up for the weed he owed for. It only took a couple of years in the weed business to figure out that the real money was to be made in dealing crack.

Half an eightball would sell for about $300 when it was broken down into rocks, sold at $10 a piece. The wholesale price: $80. A full eightball (or cube) cost about $250, and the dealer would make about $1,000 broken down.

Not a bad business to be in. Certainly paid better than any minimum-wage job a youth could find. Let alone a youth who basically dropped out in grade 9 to make this money and avoid being the stupid guy at school. Certainly helped more than the twenty bucks a day Dad gave him to live. Though he was grateful for that.

He was careful about where he dealt and who he dealt with — supplying a business card and making sure he was always available when a call came in. He also learned quickly that he needed to look after himself. He took to carrying a gun to protect the cash he made dealing.

He alternated between living in an apartment above the restaurant/booze can that dad and grandma ran and the grandmother's house. At grandma's house there were a number of crack users who would come around to do maintenance, fencing, gardening, and even flooring. They were a known clientele, so they were safe as far as dealing was concerned. Two of the crack users were living at the house with all those kids, so they became the family that wasn't otherwise around. These were the adults.

It was Tyshaun who taught Big Guy how to deal crack. Why not? It seems that Tyshaun's dad did that and ran a pretty lucrative business.

Now, while Tyshaun pretty much knew who he was dealing with, Big Guy was brasher. Big Guy liked what he saw at Tyshaun's grandma's place; there were no rules or curfews, and he wasn't made to go to church. He was pretty fond of hanging out at Tyshaun's while he pushed his own dealing.

Some of the boys in the basement of grandma's house hung up sheets around their mattresses to get a little privacy. It was on his mattress that Tyshaun's fifteen-year-old girl lost her virginity. And it was likely on this mattress she got pregnant.

Tyshaun wanted to be a good father. He was determined to be different than his father. But as Tyshaun turned sixteen, and with his girlfriend carrying his child, he was locked up on a street mugging and intimidation charge.

Tyshaun's girlfriend went to a place called Humewood House, a shelter for pregnant women. They gave her remarkable support during her pregnancy and helped her to find her own housing as she transitioned into being a mother.

When Tyshaun got out of juvenile, he went back to hustling crack. When his buddies called, he was right there for them. It didn't sit well with the mother of his child that he would just up and leave any time he felt like it. Staying at home with a kid is a drag. But out on the street and with his friends, Tyshaun thought he was getting all kinds of respect. He thought he was the man now. Certainly, girls were lining up to have sex with him and his buddies, despite the fact that he lived with his girlfriend most of the time.

He was no longer the little, lost boy with no friends, stuck in a silo.

While he loved his girlfriend and son, he was still a horny, young guy who was bedazzled by this new sense of fame and fortune — even if it was all an illusion soon to come crashing down. YDFC. Young, dumb, and full of cum.

There were a lot of friends coming in and out of his life. Tyshaun wanted to spend time with them rather than stay at home with his girlfriend and child. Street life was way more exciting. Being something of a recluse as a child, he was enjoying this sense of belonging and being wanted.

The same cycle that caught his mother led Tyshaun to street life. And street life led him to the Eaton Centre on Boxing Day 2005. He wasn't the only one caught in that cycle, not the only one brought there that day.

Tyshaun — Silo. Valentine — Short. Ralph — Big Guy. Milan — Boy. Jorrell — JoJay. There were others there that day, too. All with their own nicknames they got as kids.

Andre "Dre" Thompson's rap sheet wasn't as significant as some of the others, but he had referred to himself as a Blood from the Jungle — an area of socially assisted housing to the east of Black Creek — and had carried red bandanas consistent with gang trends in the city and throughout North America. He'd been charged with possession of cocaine and a violent street robbery where he stole designer clothing and jewellery from three young men. He was convicted on a few other accounts of assault, failure to comply, assault with intent to resist arrest, dangerous driving, failing to stop after an accident, and assault causing bodily harm. Most of those convictions came down in February 2005; he was sentenced to 250 days. So he wasn't out of jail long before the Boxing Day shooting. At the time, he had only a grade 11 education and an eighteen-month-old son who lived with his baby mama.

Dre's brother, Shaun "Speedy" Thompson, wore a one-inch gold hoop earring in his left ear. At eighteen years of age he was still in grade 12 at Weston Collegiate. He'd faced an assault charge and charges for possession of counterfeit money, but had no convictions. On Boxing Day, Speedy had "no fixed address," according to the police, although he had previously lived with his aunt and sometimes stayed with his girlfriend on Martha Eaton Way — part of Black Creek. Speedy wasn't a part of any group and his name wasn't given to him by any members of any hood. He got it at the age of six for his fast running. According to Speedy, neither his brother nor he ever owned a gun and certainly there was no evidence either did. And Speedy was a rapper and entrepreneur of sorts, having registered his own recording company, Mademen Music.

Jevoy "Jovi" Johnson lived with his mother, and there were likely problems between them as she had reported him missing on five different occasions according to Toronto Police Service records. Otherwise, Jovi was relatively clean.

Andrew "Optics" Thompson was a cousin of Tyshaun's. His major failing on Boxing Day was that he was the only one wearing anything remotely unusual — a tan-coloured suit that made him easily identifiable.

Vincent "Visa" Davis hailed from the Jane-Finch area. In his police interviews, he admitted to smoking crack and keeping his habit alive by selling it. He occasionally sported a gold cap that fit over one of his upper teeth, a signal of some form of wealth — hip-hop bling called grills if they covered more than one tooth.

Police reports indicated that Visa was running with a crowd called the Gatorz, who had replaced a self-styled Crip group on Martha Eaton Way. If Visa had, indeed, been associated with the Gatorz, he certainly wouldn't have been friends with Short, who hung with a different crowd. And if he been a member of the Gatorz, who were reported to be at war with the 5 Point Generalz, he also wouldn't have been friends with Big Guy. But he was friends with both. Here's the thing about Visa. He was friends with everyone. So if ever there would have been a peacemaker, it would have been Visa.

So much in the police reports was questionable. For starters, it was questionable whether or not the Gatorz even existed in 2005. And Big Guy was tormented by members of the 5PGs, certainly not running with them. Even Tyshaun was tormented by some of those guys.

Big Guy and Tyshaun didn't join gangs to deal with the violence, they forged friendships.

None of these guys — JoJay, Visa, Dre, Speedy, Big Guy, Tyshaun, Jovi — were members of gangs. They were friends. Andrew Thompson and Dorian Wallace were relatives. And they came together on Boxing Day just to hang out. Yes, some of them had questionable pasts. But not because they were gang members.

And the guys in Regent didn't identify their rivalries as Crips versus Bloods. The Silent Souljahs rapped about wanting to work it out and the Point Blanks rapped about the feelings of loss in Regent Park. They spoke the same language and spoke of the same pain. Now Silent Souljahs did rap "I used to keep a grudge on me/I can't deny/I still do." Because when you see your friends and brothers gunned down and know who was responsible, resentment is only natural. All because one DJ picked one group over another to play in clubs.

Members of any group can become so frustrated that they become extremists who seek retribution. And then those extremists come to paint an entire group with one broad stroke. In the Amercian Old West, William "Devil Anse" Hatfield first played off against Randolph "Ole Ran" McCoy; that personal fight became a legend. Grudges. Rivalries. Extremism.

They can exist anywhere. Up until the 1900s, vendettas were considered legal instruments. They came from the Latin origin of "vindicta" — meaning vengeance. *The Godfather* was founded upon it. Mafia rules and outlaw biker groups depend on it. Salman Rushdie faced a fatwa because he wrote *The Satanic Verses;* his execution was ordered by people who perceived that what he did was irreverent.

Rivalries. Vengeance. It's human. It's animal. Feel threatened. Freeze. Flee. Fight. Rivalries and vengeance came together Christmas night in one of the hoods.

There was this one guy from Tyshaun's neighbourhood, Richard (Richie) Steele. He was a "Blood though and through" according to his girlfriend, as well as being an "Oakwood and Vaughan" boy who dealt in drugs and weapons. He had some enemies, including Tyshaun.

Oakwood and Vaughan had a lot of self-proclaimed Bloods in its hood. In this area, 45 percent of the family incomes in 2005 were less than forty thousand dollars annually, so it was another area where poverty ran rampant. And where poverty runs in big cities, so often do drugs and guns.

The Boss Jamaican Bar on Vaughan Road was one of those places where young men gathered illegally after hours. The booze can was in the basement of a modest restaurant amidst a strip of stores including the Three Brother's restaurant, and just steps away from the First Hungarian Presbyterian Church. It was Richie's hood. It was also Tyshaun's hood.

Inconspicuous by day. Loud, dark, and dangerous by night.

Richie's mom, Valerie, was the former head of the Jamaican Canadian Association and an adjudicator with the Ontario Rental Housing Tribunal. As a prominent social activist who cared deeply about the deaths of young black men that were increasingly left uninvestigated, she would have been a strong role model for her son and a deeply concerned parent. But Richie still managed to fall in with a bad crowd, some of whom were there on Boxing Day. Valerie had spent enough heart-wrenching nights worried about the crowd her son was running with, the defiance he was exhibiting at home, and, as a strong advocate for racial equality, how he was letting down his people by becoming a thug.

On the night of Christmas Day, 2005, it went down like this:

Tyshaun hears there are guys looking for him at the booze can. So he goes down there with a buddy. Tyshaun's uncle sees him in the haze of smoke and the dark atmosphere where Tyshaun is trying to stay on the down low. His uncle, who was in and out of jail.

"Silo!" His uncle yells out.

Lots of heads turn. Tyshaun's head turns, but so does Richie's.

Tyshaun's buddy said it was time to get out of there, so they took the back exit, only to be followed by Richie and a couple of his buddies. They hit the top of the stairs and Tyshaun opened the door, but turned around to face Richie, lifting his shirt to reveal his weapon. Richie wasn't ready for that and backed down.

It seems that Richie, in addition to his allegiance to the Vaughan Road Bloods, also had friends in the Five Point Generalz, members of whom allegedly both terrorized Tyshaun and his friends, dissed Tyhshaun's girlfriend on numerous occasions, came at him with guns, had him framed for gun theft, and then eventually had him "jumped" inside the Don Jail. The same 5PGs who the cops thought Big Guy was part of.

Big Guy was not a part of a gang. But he was gonna watch out for his friend Tyshaun.

6

Raining in Toronto

I've been so cold and wondering when it's gonna get
  better.
And though I've been told that the sun won't always
  shine in bad weather
But can somebody explain why it's always raining in
  Toronto
My hustle to survive lights my way feeling like it's
  always raining in Toronto.
— Frankie Payne, "Raining in Toronto"

In Toronto, on Boxing Day 2005, it wasn't raining. There was some slush on the ground. That's thicker than rain. There was the threat of blood. That's thicker than water.

And it was thick.

Shoes can make noise. Walking can echo for years. You might choose tap shoes to replicate Fred Astaire moves, or high heels to click power, or slippers to sneak, or high-tops to speak. With the exception of army boots, shoes are meant for leisure, work, or sport. Not for killing.

Remember this sound: voices rebounding off the pavement and sidewalks — some, the homeless asking for change; some, the outrages of a dispute; some, brazen teens singing in a drunken stupor; most, just the idle conversations of people walking to and from the various points in their lives. A constant white noise of cars travelling, of taxis honking, of subways rumbling underfoot, and, about every ten minutes, a siren echoing. It's just another dusk in Toronto. With the exception of the odd Christmas carol sneaking out of a store.

But if you listened very closely, there was poetry that could tell stories of plights, of fights, of sorrows, of time borrowed. Of rivalries, heated up by the previous night's heat about to turn into fire.

On Boxing Day, from various locations around the city, some friends and rivals came together down at the Eaton Centre.

JoJay had been staying at his brother's place in the Jane-Finch neighbourhood. He went to see his mother; she didn't have heat or water working over Christmas, and he wanted to help her out. After, he headed down to the Eaton Centre to meet up with Big Guy. Dre and Speedy joined, as well as Visa and Optics, Tyshaun's cousin.

On Yonge Street late that afternoon, they spotted Richie.

When Big Guy saw Richie on the street, he said to his friends, "There's that Vaughan guy." Richie had come after Tyshaun the night before and had previously had altercations with both Tyshaun and Big Guy in the Vaughan neighbourhood. JoJay sprang into action and sucker-punched Richie, then stole his cellphone and some cash. Richie couldn't fight back. His arm was in a sling because he had recently been shot.

The jury at the trial of JoJay would never hear that he was the one who jumped Richie and stole his cellphone and about two hundred bucks that afternoon. Even if the public may think that's good cause to show that JoJay was a "bad dude," the courts don't see it that way. Just because he was involved in the cellphone theft didn't make him a shooter. And the courts couldn't call up Richie's history to show how he might have been involved. That would make the telling of the story way too complicated. Got to keep things as simple as possible for a jury.

Instead, the prosecution wanted to say that because Richie was a friend of Short's, this "gang" that JoJay and Big Guy were hanging with was targeting both Short and Richie's "gang."

Not so easy. After the cellphone theft, more people affiliated both with Richie and JoJay started showing up down at the Eaton Centre. JoJay just wanted to hook up with his girlfriend, but he didn't want to be alone down there; it's way too scary to be out on your own when you know there are people looking for you. He wanted his buddy Dre to just stay with him and leave the rest of the guys to go their own ways. But Dre wanted to stay with his brother, Speedy. Peer pressure.

Tyshaun and his cousin from England, Dorian Wallace, had been at a mall close to their home. They were there with another friend named Kory Benoit Jones, the same Kory with the smoking room and the sometimes roommate Big Guy. Kory, it seems, didn't want to go to the Eaton Centre. But they decided they would head downtown anyway. Patricia gave her son and cousin a lift. She was surprised Dorian wanted to go along. And why were they going? Was it because Tyshaun had heard about Richie being down there and the altercation?

JoJay didn't even know Tyshaun. He just knew that he was someone Big Guy knew. He would have had no idea that Tyshaun and Richie had previously had dealings, even as recently as the wee hours of that morning. He wouldn't even have known the reason he jumped Richie was because of those dealings. Tyshaun and Dorian just joined in with the group.

After the cellphone incident, one of Tyshaun's closest friends also headed down to the Eaton Centre, "White Choco." He was one of those white guys who desperately wanted to be black, politely called, in some circles, "whiggers" — just like Boy. Choco had always been a good boy and rarely got into trouble. His escape drug was the slow easy buzz of a joint. He didn't fancy anything stronger to take him away from his worries. He was the same guy who was at the booze can the night before. He was the one who told Tyshaun they needed to get out of there rather than face Richie's wrath. Choco didn't like altercations.

It wasn't long after the cellphone theft on Yonge Street that another incident occurred. This time it was inside the Eaton Centre. Who knows why Choco decided to fight a guy outside the H&M store inside the Eaton Centre; maybe because he saw Big Guy as the man. Big Guy had made it pretty clear to others that he was packing, even if he never showed them the gun he had stashed. He was milling about in the Eaton Centre with his right arm outside of his coat sleeve the whole time. It was a way people who are carrying can easily adjust the two pounds or so of metal shifting around their waist. Maybe Choco had the fight because of his loyalty to Tyshaun, who he perceived as facing trouble. Who was the guy Choco took on? It's still not clear, but it was certainly someone who knew Short. Could have been Eric Boateng, Jermaine Osbourne, or Anthony Moodie, all associates of Short's, but all killed not that long after the incidents of the day.

JoJay was the one to step in and calm things down. He was the one who told the others to just walk away. He was the one who wanted the escalation to stop. After all, JoJay was under house arrest and wasn't even supposed to be out. The fistfight lasted maybe thirty seconds. No weapons at the time. Just guys who thought they needed to prove their point, trying to prove their point. But the fight was one more reason to be getting some hate on after the cellphone beating. Alphas taking on alphas. JoJay knew that Short would hear he broke up the fight and that he wanted to keep the peace. It turns out Short was something of an affiliate of JoJay's on the music scene. JoJay's uncle was a member of the Point Blank rap crew while Short was a supporter of Silent Souljahs. JoJay knew that being seen as a peacekeeper was essential between these two groups.

Richie wasn't there for the fight. He had gone to another part of Toronto shopping for shoes with his girlfriend after he got robbed, but he kept repeating to her that he wanted to go back to the Eaton Centre, while his girlfriend pleaded that he not. So Richie and his girlfriend headed home, but after a while he got antsy about missing out on potential action back at the Eaton Centre.

Meanwhile, Short and Boy had arrived from their Boxing Day party in Regent Park. They got out of their cab just east of the Eaton Centre; even if it was Christmas, you could always find a few crackheads in that neighbourhood. Boy made some deals and pocketed the cash. Since Short was his man, he likely saw a cut. After, they made their way over to the Eaton Centre and the Footlocker store to check out shoes.

Nobody was sure why Richie was back there when the gunshots rang out. Was it because he had a beef with Tyshaun and Big Guy? More likely it was because he knew Short was down there and knew he had a friend and protector in him. Richie may have even got word about the fight that happened inside the Eaton Centre and figured there was strength in numbers. Not gangs. Just guys confused about the concept of loyalty. Tempers were heating up, and like most boys are taught at a young age, you never back down from a bully. Go head-to-head, regardless of the consequences. Because you're a wimp if you back down and choose peace.

If these guys were really in gangs, they would have been more organized, and clearer about who was on which side. It was hardly a case of *West Side Story* or Bloods and Crips. It was more about boys trying to be what they thought men were made of; something very few of them had personal experience with as most of their fathers were absentee at best, dead at worst — or maybe just in and out of jail themselves.

All this came together as the friends and rivals gathered at the Eaton Centre. The two "groups" headed outside of the Eaton Centre. JoJay got a look at Eric "Boderick" Boateng and began to rail Boderick while out on Yonge Street. "Who's this guy thinking he's all that?" JoJay was reported to say. It didn't take long for that heat to crank up as JoJay, Big Guy, Short, and Boy, along with some female friends, went into a shoe store. Lots of dissing. Screw-facing (dirty looks). Primarily Big Guy screw-facing Boy, as Big Guy had apparently said something along the line of "nice necklace" to Boy, who interpreted this as a threat. These were the menacing eyes of guys who had seen so much violence growing up that their souls were buried somewhere so deep they didn't dare share that they had one. A life on the streets wasn't much different than army training — you end up seeing enemies, not human beings. Short and Boy decided they needed to get out of the store to stay safe. They figured there was far less likely to be trouble out on Yonge Street than in the store.

Tyshaun and Richie. JoJay and Boderick. But the real beef as they exited the shoe store was between Short and Big Guy. Short wanted to know why Visa's friend, Big Guy, was screw-facing Boy. Or maybe he wanted to know why JoJay was railing Broderick. Visa said there wasn't a problem. Seems Short didn't believe him.

Short wouldn't come up short; Big Guy wouldn't come up big.

Jane Creba was out shopping that day with her sister Alison. Jane was just crossing the street to go to the Pizza Pizza to use the bathroom. The Pizza Pizza was right beside the Footlocker. Jane wouldn't have been aware that there was a stare down happening nearby. Hot looks between Short and Big Guy, and Short knew Big Guy had a gun. At the trial, the experts who trained police on gun carrying offered up their interpretation: Big Guy's arm was outside of his sleeve because he was holding. Short didn't need a police expert to tell him that. He had real experience in the hood. When Short saw Visa outside the store, he asked him straight up. "Why's your boy screw-facing my boy?"

Visa said it was all cool. He tried to calm things down. But it wasn't working. Short wasn't convinced anything was cool.

Now, just a few steps outside of the Footlocker and a very short distance from Big Guy, Short let it be known that he wasn't going to take any more shit. There he was standing along with the other Regent Park guys, Boderick and Jermaine Osbourne (J9). Boy was obviously there. Richie too.

Facing northbound on Yonge Street, Short had words. "Who's your boy? This is *my* boy," Short yelled as he waved his hand, revealing to the onlookers the shiny tip of a gun inside his sleeve. Was he referring to Boy, Richie, the guy who was jumped inside the Eaton Centre, or to Boateng, who JoJay was mouthing off to? After he said "this is my boy" a series of numbers was yelled.

Apparently, his boy was his .357 Ruger.

Facing southbound, Big Guy did what he thought he needed to do and showed Short that he wasn't the only armed man there. One of the men near Big Guy yelled back, "Fuck this shit."

Then shots rang out. That's it.

Cuss words that never should have gone further.

Jane was just crossing the street. She was *just* crossing the street. The first of Short's shots took Jane down by the curb. Short missed his real target. Big Guy didn't duck or fire back. It seems he took the third option when faced by a probable death. He froze.

In a split second, JoJay grabbed the now petrified Big Guy's 9-millimetre and fired back, although not aiming directly at anyone or thing. Someone hit Dorian Wallace and blew a hole in his chest. Eventually, an informant would say it was Jermaine Osborne (J9) who "emptied at Dorian." Jermaine wouldn't live to be tried for that assault. He was the one Creedy eventually killed.

The 9-millimetre hit Boy in the leg. As the groups hurriedly tried to retreat, pulling each other backwards, Tyshaun fired once (with his eyes closed) before his gun jammed. His spent casing was found close by on the ground, so he hadn't hit anyone. It seems most of the guys who fired guns were too frightened to fire into the crowd, so they instead fired down towards the ground.

When the first bullet was fired, there was confusion as people began to ask if that was gunfire. Mass panic struck when they realized it was. Most ran away, those too close scurried for cover and screamed for help as Dorian fell in the middle of the street and Jane slumped on a nearby curb. The only people directly involved in the shooting to get hit were Boy and Jovi. Boy didn't realize he was hit until he was several blocks away and his legs stopped working. Jovi tried to run, but went down fast and hard on the street.

Three bystanders were struck by shrapnel — an off-duty police officer named David Audette, and two women out shopping that day. They all slipped to the side of the street when they realized they'd been struck. Everyone else ran in whatever direction they could.

The entire shootout lasted mere seconds. The lead-up took years.

JoJay and Dre fled on foot before hailing a cab. Dorian Wallace was attended to by an off-duty medic, but somehow managed to get up and, with the help of his cousin, Andrew "Optics" Smith, they took a cab to St. Michael's Hospital nearby, where the "man in the tan suit" dropped him off and headed straight to his girlfriend's place.

Jovi was helped by some of the girls there. Calls went out to 911, and ambulance personnel came to tend to him.

Big Guy, Tyshaun, Visa, and Speedy all stuck together. They took a cab back to the Black Creek area — to Kory's crib — where they turned on Toronto's all-news television station, CP24.

Big Guy kicked Kory out of his own place after (per Kory's reports) Big Guy said "I hope I didn't hit her," and "I hope Jevoy is okay." Later, Kory told the jury that Tyshaun said, "I fired off my whole clip." Tyshaun's whole clip? Hardly.

Regardless of who shot what, all of the young men were in shock. Yes, they had guns. But they didn't expect to use them. Why carry when your only intent is to scare others and never use it? They carried guns because they thought if they did, they wouldn't have to face up to violence. Pre-emptive prevention; having a gun would prevent anyone else from using theirs. An arms race as old as time, on a smaller scale.

The media would tell us about Jane, and a bit about the bystanders hit by shrapnel. Not so much about Dorian, Jovi, and Boy. Out of respect for Jane's family, the media would almost exclusively present one picture of Jane — a black-and-white family photo. We would not see the carnage, and we would not see images of the life she lived prior to this tragedy.

The whole experience could be boiled down to basic photography. A positive allows a record that tries to replicate what we see. A negative is a latent image that needs greater exposure.

What we saw in all the media accounts was the beautiful smile of a young woman, and the scowling faces of black men's mug shots. Positives and negatives. All of those black guys brought together on Boxing Day through some very common experiences: poverty, addiction, poor social housing, racism, poor decisions.

As Big Guy, Tyshaun, Speedy, and Visa watched on the television in Kory's crib, the announcement came that Jane had been pronounced dead on arrival at St. Michael's Hospital.

A gunshot wound to the torso with a perforating injury to the aorta.

7

The Hunt

April is the cruelest month, breeding
Lilacs out of the dead land, mixing
Memory and desire, stirring
Dull roots with spring rain.
Winter kept us warm, covering
Earth in forgetful snow, feeding
A Little life with dried tubers.
— T.S. Eliot, *The Waste Land*[1]

Detective Savas Kyriacou was a tall, soft-spoken family man with the hint of a Greek accent who had served decades in the police force before becoming a lead in the homicide department. He was leaving his home with his wife and three children to attend a family event when he received the phone call on Boxing Day. Family plans were put on hold. He quickly made calls to line up his eight key investigators, and then arranged to meet his partner, Detective Brian Borg, at the scene.

By the time Kyriacou arrived, JoJay had been caught at the Castle Frank subway station with his pal Dre. Their cabbie had overheard a phone conversation, and with all those sirens going, and these guys very tense, he thought it best to report their plans. JoJay and Dre were met by the police force at the subway station where JoJay had intended to meet with his girlfriend. Both JoJay and Dre were taken into custody. JoJay had a gun in his pocket.

The news only ever reported that fifty police officers got involved with the case.[2] In fact, there were over a hundred … certainly more officers than had ever been involved in a gun homicide involving an innocent victim caught in "gang war." Was it because it happened on Boxing Day? Was it because it didn't happen in a hood? Or was it….

"You never think anything is going to happen on Boxing Day," Kyriacou said to reporters.

Well, you don't expect this outside a hood, but you might expect it inside. Or you might expect domestic-related homicides in a time that is supposed to be full of peace but often deviates into a hard escalation of family stress. But Kyriacou was right that you wouldn't expect gunfire on a busy street full of shoppers.

The police didn't live in the hoods like Marz or Short or Big Guy — knowing that any day could be a bad day even before it started.

Kyriacou and his team had a lot of shit to deal with. It was mayhem. Kyriacou needed to set up his team and gather as much information as possible, as quickly as possible — evidence left for a few days can easily be corrupted. They needed to gather everything they could. According to Kyriacou's report, "The first few days are very, very important. Time passes. You lose evidence. You lose forensics. You lose witnesses. That's why it was important to get the resources, manpower, right away."[3]

The investigation started in the traditional ways. Cordon off the area. Label everything found on the street, from shell casings to hats. Label exactly who was hit where. The shell casings left behind were those of a 9-millimetre (Big Guy's, but not shot by him), a 38-millimetre (Short's), and a 25-millimetre (Tyshaun's). There was a bullet lodged in Jovi's leg, but for some reason, the investigators never looked into which gun had fired into Jovi. Why not? Was it because it was from another gun? (Even many years later, the judges hearing the appeals wondered why that hadn't been investigated.) So, despite there being so many men there that day with so many potential guns, only Tyshaun's, Big Guy's, and Short's were the ones identified as having been fired.

Kyriacou had to collect any witnesses he could too. Since it was Boxing Day on Yonge Street, there were a lot of people to interview, and most of them were in shock. But Kyriacou needed to get the freshest memories. What did you see? We can try to identify them later, just tell me what you saw and heard.

What did they see and hear? What became clear from the beginning was that it was black men yelling at each other before the shots rang out.

The loss of Jane Creba struck a definite chord for Kyriacou. He had a lot in common with the Creba family. They both hailed from the Toronto's Danforth area, and were from solid, hard-working, Greek immigrant families. In the case of Jane's family, her mom was a teacher and her dad an architect. Kyriacou had children about the same age as Jane. Ones he was raising to be solid citizens. Ones nobody would want gunned down in a senseless act of violence.

The public felt the same affinity for Jane. People posted online about the loss of innocence when a sweet young woman gets gunned down by a bunch of thugs. She was popular, athletic, scholarly, and promising. She was just shopping. It could have been any of our kids. It could have been Kyriacou's kid.

In the days after the shooting, the outpouring of tributes in the form of flowers and cards left near the Eaton Centre was unmatched by any other homicide site in Toronto's history. Her death meant more than any of the other homicides that year. Because it was Christmas. Because it wasn't supposed to happen outside of the projects. And, frankly, because she was a white girl.

Kyriacou tirelessly pursued the many leads and misleads with a photograph and a painting of the late Jane posted on his wall throughout his investigation.

With tips flowing in to various hotlines, victims and witnesses needing to be interviewed, evidence from the crime site to be gathered, and forensics to be processed — not to mention those two guys captured at the subway station — it was not just mayhem on the streets that day, but mayhem all through the early days of the investigation.

The police had intelligence that suggested there were some gang wars going on in the city before the Boxing Day shooting; they figured that was likely a part of the puzzle.

But how to make sense of the senseless?

Police investigations don't happen chronologically. First you interview this guy, then you sort through these forensics, then you try to get something from informants. An investigation happens in a coordinated way, rapidly and with remarkable strategy. A cosmos of information dumped into an elaborate system intended to sort, search, and refine.

Most sources that come into police prove futile, leading to hours of investigation that yield little. But sometimes a source comes through to provide the clarity needed.

There were a key few in the Creba case: JoJay, in custody with one of the guns. And then, out of nowhere, Marz, who made a phone call to Crime Stoppers. Some of the first informants said talk to Kevin Smith, aka Nem-S-Sis, who was a well-established rapper from the Jane-Finch neighbourhood.

But Nem-S-Sis didn't talk. Seems if he knew anything, it was only by way of word on the street, and he wasn't going to get involved when he didn't need to be. He was determined to make it out of the ghetto with his rap and he didn't need to mess up what was going well in his life. As he told it to interviewers about his music, he "did the talk … not the shit" — meaning that while his rap lyrics reflected the surroundings he grew up in, where violence and survival were key, he had zero interest in any gang activities. He just passed on their words and some advice to them via his lyrics.

The rapper's name probably came up because he was connected with all of these guys and all of their pithy rivalries. He was one of the guys who could put the rivalries aside in order to inspire people to be creative and find their way out of the hood. The thugs trusted him to speak something of their experiences. The thing is, he was a sounding board for musical experiences to take their stories out. He was a storyteller. Not a rat. Not a thug. Just a guy who made music out of suffering and hope. He had the bigger picture — he didn't get hung up on stupid shit, didn't get hung up on individual grudges and instead fought the bigger systems that were keeping young African Canadians down.

But it's way easier to challenge an individual than a system, because systems don't have faces. They have entrenched policies, histories, and narratives that you can't just shoot at when you are frustrated and maybe failed by education. If you don't have education and confidence, you might not know that all institutions, policies, beliefs, and systems are as organic as people. They are born. Their life may be sustained. They may die young. Or they may rise to prominence before they eventually die. It's just that institutions and systems often have much longer lifespans than people. Some institutions last years. Some decades. Some thousands of years. But they all eventually die. Real artists understand this. They understand that they live within a system that will change if they keep pushing back and throwing questions out. Eventually.

Nem-S-Sis wasn't the guy to try to get information out of. He was one of the rappers trying to make things right. He was one of the many artists in Toronto who understood that you can't shoot holes in people to fix a systemic problem.

But the police had someone they could try to get information out of immediately. JoJay, caught with a gun, was in trouble. But he certainly wasn't ratting that first night he was interviewed. He merely said he was passed one of the guns after the shooting because he was a young offender. JoJay said the guy who passed it figured he should be the one holding the "smoking gun" because he wouldn't face the same penalties as the guy who passed it. As he told the cops, "If you guys, if you guys even check the fingerprints on the clip, on the trigger finger you'll find someone else. You would find my fingerprints probably like on the, on the trigger, on the handle, on the handle. But if you check the clip you'll see someone else's handprints on it. It's just that I had it in my pocket already when everything was done."[4] He didn't mention any names, but he was letting them know they might find his DNA on the trigger.

When the big days of interviews came along on January 1 and 2, JoJay started to say a little more about who was there with him that day. It was pretty obvious that the police were going to find out exactly who was there anyway; they let JoJay know there were cameras all around the Eaton Centre. JoJay started to get an idea of how much they already knew when they asked about Big Guy. Interestingly, JoJay said that he had known Big Guy for about ten years, but that he didn't really like him anymore. "He's an acquaintance," JoJay explained. "I would — I used to talk to him, you know, like when I was younger I was close to him, but then I just broke away from him, because I didn't like the way he was."[5]

Kyriacou, conducting the interview, said, "Tell us about him. What do you know about Ralph [Big Guy]? Is he a good guy? Is he a bad guy? Is he any different guy? Tell us — is he an intellectual? Tell us about him. What do you know about him, you've known him for a long time?"

JoJay just said, "I don't know if like I couldn't put any — I don't know cause I couldn't — I don't know the answer to that question."

The truth was Big Guy called the shots on where people were going that day. And since it was Boxing Day in a big mall where enemies could be anywhere, JoJay thought it best to follow along with the group, as opposed to just staying put and waiting for his girlfriend. Big Guy was the one who seemed to know trouble was coming, as JoJay reported that Big Guy told those with him, "We need to stick together. Everything will be cool." According to JoJay, Big Guy "had that attitude like 'No one could fuck with us right now.'" JoJay took it to mean that Big Guy was packing.[6]

And, as JoJay told it to his interviewers, there were people out there who wouldn't think twice about killing JoJay for some of his past stupid actions.

He felt comfortable being downtown with his buddy Dre — not so much Big Guy, but Dre wanted to stay with his brother, Speedy, who was travelling with Big Guy.

Eventually some further information would come from JoJay. His uncle who was in the rap group Point Blank had put out a recording of JoJay's called "Me and You." And lo and behold, the studio where JoJay recorded his song was run by a guy named Nem-S-Sis — the very same rap artist police tried to get information out of based on some bad leads.

Small world. It seemed that JoJay knew both Point Blank and Nem-S-Sis.

When the investigators suggested that Point Blank wasn't a rap group, but a gang, JoJay was clear: "Point Blank Soldiers is something that cops made up.... That is something that never existed."[7]

When pressed about where the investigators could get a copy of JoJay's song, he reported that nobody could get it. "No. I'd rather make a record label buy it.... And [not] let the world listen to it and not make no money off it. That's what a lot of the Canadian artists do. That's why they're nowhere."

JoJay's version of events was that Big Guy fired the gun, and then handed it to him afterward. So why would JoJay also tell the cops that he hadn't handled the gun otherwise, but that they might find his DNA on the trigger? Not on the clip. But on the trigger. Why on the trigger if he hadn't fired it? When JoJay told his story in his statements to the police, he admitted that he didn't duck or try to run during the gunfire … something that would be an automatic response. He stood straight up, right beside Big Guy.

Why not duck? He was told forthright by the interrogator: "You didn't duck because you were busy shooting." JoJay denied that. Just said it all happened so fast that he didn't think to duck.

But does someone "think" about dodging bullets?

8

Rap, Rats, and the G-code

Was it individuals or gangs? The police were getting different stories from everyone. Pieces and puzzles. Who brought their pieces downtown that day? How would the cops ever figure it out with the G-code working against them?

The cops would eventually get information from the guys who wanted out; those who were willing to talk in the hopes of finding a better life. But it was awfully confusing and time consuming with all the different names coming forward. Most wouldn't talk; at least thirty of the men tapped for information refused to say a thing. Who were the men who would speak? Who would want to get out?

Putting the story together was tough besides. Everyone had opinions, different perspectives, different biases. The police thought the shooting was gang related right from the start. JoJay said it wasn't. He tried to teach the cops about rap artists and how challenging it was to find your way as one. He tried to tell the police that their theories about gangs were wrong.

But the police didn't listen; they remained focused on gangs — west-end guys against Regent Park. One early source that came in to the police seemed to confirm that. He reported that he knew there were two "groups" involved. He claimed there was a West End "gang" duking it out with some guys from Regent Park. The source mentioned men in the "West End Gang" — Big Guy and Silo — but who was shooting back? He didn't know. Nobody was talking about Short. And who was this white guy showing up at a restaurant near the shooting who wound up with a bullet in his leg? Did JoJay fire a gun? Was he, in fact, the "first guy to shoot," as some claimed? He was, after all, found with the smoking gun just minutes after the shootings. A lot didn't make sense to the police, despite all the information coming in. The police would need to find a few more guys who didn't follow the G-code. A few more guys who would rat out their friends for easier sentences. A few more guys to explain the grudges.

There was Creedy, who was big in the Regent Park hood and well known to the police because he had a lot of guys already snitching to the cops *about* him. How about trying to get information out of him? He seemed to have a pretty high profile. There was also Marz, who wanted an end to bloodshed. And there was Kory, whose DNA was on one of the guns. He could be made to talk. And there were a few other guys who could be excused if they stepped up — namely Short and Richie. But those testimonies wouldn't come easily.

Marz came forward early, not first. A couple of days after his friends returned from the Boxing Day shooting, Marz had more information than he could stomach. He thought his call to Crime Stoppers was going to be anonymous. He thought it might help to stop some of the bloodshed and might stop some of the misinformation that was being presented in the media about rival gangs in his neighbourhood. He knew there were no rival gangs, just misunderstandings between individuals. But those misunderstandings were far too nuanced for a media focused on presenting the impoverished, young black men as anything but belonging to a human race where issues collide and ideologies are conflicted. Sadly, these were individuals who had issues, and it was far easier to present the nuances as "gang warfare."

In his call to Crime Stoppers, according to the court documents, Marz said, "And I correct them in saying it's not as spontaneous as the media is trying to make it seem. It wasn't no gang shootout. There wasn't two factions that seen each other and they start blazing."

On the Crime Stoppers tip sheet for informants the following would have been what Marz understood:

> Crime Stoppers does not want to know who you are. We do not subscribe to "Call Display," "Call Trace," record phone conversations, or take any action that may identify you, the caller. When you call, you will be given a confidential code number. Do not, under any circumstances, give that number to anyone else. This is the only way we can link you to your tip information. Depending on the information and crime, you will be asked to call back at certain intervals to obtain an update on your information. Since we do not know you, or your phone number, YOU have to initiate any contact with us.

Do not use a cellphone when calling as these calls could be monitored by scanners. Use a secure land line number to call 1-800-222-8477.

Word on the street was that there was a fifty-thousand-dollar reward for anyone who provided a tip that led to an arrest. It wasn't true, and certainly Marz wasn't calling to claim any sort of reward; he was calling because he wanted the bloodshed to end. Nobody got any money for snitching.

The cops got information from a few others, namely Short himself, despite his warning others (including Vincent "Visa" Davis) to respect the G-code. And later, Kory Benoit-James who would do all he could in court to show that Big Guy was a big-time shooter.

Another regular confidential informant was GaYves Gandwimbi, who was ready to rat out someone from Regent Park. He had already assisted the cops with two other murders, so some of the guys from Regent Park were looking to "lick down" Yves if they found him. On the street, that meant murder him.

Yves singled out Eric Boateng as having a gun on Boxing Day. But Yves didn't know Eric had already provided hearsay witness information to the police — snitching just like Gandwimbi was.

Eric didn't make it to trial. He wasn't even put in prison, even though he was a suspect. Instead, he would get "called down" and killed outside the infamous Don Jail. What's a calldown? Eric was asked by someone to come and visit him in jail. The guys who wanted him dead arranged that meeting so they would know where he was that day and took him out, probably because they thought he would rat or had heard that he already was. Nobody was ever charged for his murder.

Anthony Moodie was also reportedly there on Boxing Day, but he would only ever face charges of drug possession. Anyway, he likely didn't have a gun; just in the wrong place at the wrong time — if he was even there. Still, his mug shot was splashed in the newspapers in connection with the Creba murder. People reading the news judged right then that he was a big, black shooter. And when people from the hood saw that he was "connected" to the events, some may have thought he would prove to be a threat as a rat. He was gunned down in the Jane-Finch area. He wouldn't go to trial. Nor would his murderer.

Gandwimbi was given protective custody and relocated in the middle of the night. The police had to get him out of Toronto because there was a price on his head. But then he refused to testify. That's a big no-no. Eventually connected to a first-degree murder that took place in November 2005 that the police didn't know about when they moved him out of Toronto, Gandwimbi went the way of most snitches. He was stabbed to death in Montreal in what was called a "botched home-invasion."

Moodie. Boateng. Gandwimbi. Leads the police tried to follow, all murdered. And there certainly wasn't a lot of work done to try to find out who killed those guys. So, if you're inside a hood and know that your life matters less than someone who doesn't live inside a hood, why would you try to help the police?

Other informants came forward. Most were cautious and wouldn't speak. Why would you say anything when you saw your brothers go down only because there was word on the street that they were being tapped for information? Tapped on the shoulder. Brought in for a chat. The taps were turned on, but so were the plugs. Some of those plugs were slugs. Street term for bullets. Put two in your chest.

The media reports, the informants, all the heat around the shootings, it all put others at risk. Marz's brother was in the Don Jail on Boxing Day. Not even involved in the shooting, Marz and his brother were somehow brought into it and would face the threats of plugs and slugs. Plug someone — put a bullet in them. Slug someone — take them down.

Eric Boateng was killed outside the Don Jail. Prisons are dangerous both inside and out.

The Don, as it was known before it was closed, wasn't a place anyone would want to be. Sewage, rats, guys crammed in three to a cell that was meant to hold one. Even prison guards had walked off the job there because the conditions were so brutal; the smells, rancid reminders of over 150 years of sweat and feces. And the remains of the gallows from the prison's earlier days reminding criminals that many had been hanged there, that some of the men who'd been hanged there were unsuccessfully hanged and wound up dying by decapitation, that some of the men previously imprisoned chose to swan-dive off the third-floor balcony of the prison to their death. That so many men committed suicide in many other ways rather than die in this hellhole.

Twenty-six men were hanged there, including three double hangings, the last of which was in 1962.

Perhaps its spectacular gargoyles on the façade and intricately detailed snakes and dragons designed in iron on the inner architecture that met anyone who was entering would elicit an appreciation of art. It was, instead, a welcome to Hades.

In a 2003 ruling, the justice system found that the jail didn't even meet the "Standard Minimum Rules for the Treatment of Prisoners" as set out by the United Nations. Dilapidated was an understatement. Even the "new wing" of the Don Jail was a hellhole that seemed to be from a different time. And it housed people who had no conviction; people who were just awaiting trial.

It wasn't until 2009, when a handful of press photographers were invited in to photograph the facility, that anyone would understand just how horrific the conditions were.

The police tried to get information out of some of the guys inside the jail right after the shootings. Some of them would talk, just for the chance to get out. But those on the inside got a lot wrong because they were only listening to the street talk. They were saying what they heard, that's all. They didn't have the real information from the streets.

Marz's brother was in the Don that day. But he certainly wouldn't be talking. Eric went there just visiting. Eventually he wouldn't be able to talk.

Marz had lived with all of this violence all of his life and he had become sick and tired of it. He was tired of watching people go to jail, people deported, people die, people heated up by a frustration with systems that were oversimplified into personal rivalries. He wanted all of this to end. He had faith that he could make some sort of a change.

Here's what Marz could tell the police:

He was at home on Boxing Day, watching his soap opera after his brother's friends headed downtown where all the real drama was going down. A split screen came on just as the show ended. On one side of the screen were the show's credits, on the other side was the news of the shooting at the Eaton Centre. He knew Boy and Short were there.

He saw from the footage that Boy was hurt. Marz tried numerous times to call him. When Short and Boy saw Marz a couple of days later, they had a lot to share about what had happened. Marz took a few days to think over what he heard before he made the decision to call in.

Now, Marz was no angel by any means. He had a long record that included attempted murder and drug dealing. But, according to him, it was one thing to pop off at guys in the hood, it was another to take it to the streets and rob an innocent young woman of her life. Some thugs grow up. They mature. They somehow gain a conscience. Maybe that's what brought Marz to make the call to Crime Stoppers.

Once Marz started talking, things happened quickly. The police had names. Short. Boy. Big Guy.

The police learned from Marz that there was heat between the Silent Souljahs and Point Blank/TnT.[1] The TnT/Point Blank and Silent Souljahs rivalry made some sense, in the context of neighbourhood rivalry; but in the grand scheme, it didn't make sense for the rivalries on Boxing Day. The media would never dive into the sort of investigative journalism that would expose the dissonance between actual testimonials (there were no gangs) and crown theories (there were two gangs). Instead, news outlets boiled the shooting down into an easily digestible story. That's not the fault of the reporters. Investigative journalism is expensive and doesn't sell.

The media just kept putting mug shots up in the papers and on television. And kept putting up the photo of Jane Creba alongside those mug shots.

Eventually, the media would tell it the way it made sense: Silent Souljahs and Point Blank "Soldiers." Even if Point Blank Soldiers didn't exist as a gang, and Point Blank was only a rap group. It was way easier to develop a prosecution case that involved gangs, and for reporters to report it that way.

Wiretaps were authorized and more information started coming in. On March 10, a newspaper reported that arrests were imminent and close. Visa got a call that day from none other than Short (who called himself Shackles in that call) to say he and his friends had better respect the G-code. It was a great deal of good fortune for the investigators to find out that he had been at the Boxing Day shooting. And to know that Visa knew Short.

Visa was the one who tried to settle things down outside the Footlocker. No credit there. Wiretaps placed on his phone eventually revealed he was wearing the tan suit, the one he sold for a hundred dollars in March after news was hitting the papers and the streets about it.

Reports also came in on Big Guy.

Shortly after Boxing Day, the cops put a trace on Big Guy. It wasn't long before they tracked him down "bigging up" his rep as one of the shooters, driving dangerously, and still carrying guns. Within just two weeks of the Creba shooting, the police reported that he robbed a family business with a shotgun, making off with twelve cartons of cigarettes in the companionship of two other men. The owners were beaten.

Or so said the police files. The reality was quite different.

The shop was actually a front for selling drugs, and it was three other people who robbed the store, not two. The owner didn't show up in court because he would have had to explain that it wasn't actually cigarettes that were stolen, and it wasn't actually Big Guy who did the stealing. So it was thrown out of court. But still in Big Guy's police files.

On January 17, drug squad officers made some crack cocaine buys from Big Guy and Tyshaun. The next day, they were placed under arrest. By all reports in the media, the police were still uncertain who the "northbound" shooters were, but they had Big Guy and Tyshaun pegged as the southbound shooters.

During the arrest, Big Guy allegedly rammed several police vehicles in an attempt to flee, even sending one of the officers to hospital.

Photos his father took of the car after the arrest tell a way different story.

It was Big Guy's car that was T-boned and totalled during the arrest. But he was required to pay two thousand dollars to the police for damaging their car, even if by all photographic evidence they were the ones who rammed him and wrote off his car. No stories or files would ever disclose this. No investigation would be called.

A search warrant executed at his girlfriend's residence shortly after this arrest turned up a .32-calibre revolver and ammunition. This was despite a previous court order that Big Guy was prohibited from possessing a firearm. The problem? He didn't live with his girlfriend; he lived with his parents and worked in his community with needy children. He played baseball. He went to church every Sunday. Was it his gun? Who knows? Police notes don't require that evidence is proven before it is inserted into files.

His rap sheets were a huge source of worry because often the stories told in them were heavily one-sided, and certainly not in Big Guy's favour.

Rap sheets. Sometimes they helped police track down offenders, sometimes they were fiction. Big Guy armed and dangerous. No. Big Guy member of 5PGz violent gang. No.

Big Guy's dad was the poet called Rapper. His spoken word poetry questioned discrimination through rhyme and reason. Home life clearly wasn't the cause of Big Guy's problems. But still, Big Guy carried a gun that day downtown. In fact, he wanted to have a second gun with him, but his other gun was being used that day by a guy who would eventually turn against him as an informant — his then-roommate, Kory Benoit James.

Guys who deal crack more often than not carry guns. Even though he carried a gun that day, it seems Big Guy wasn't as tough as he wanted others to think. He just felt like he needed to have big attitude, and that big attitude was likely a significant contribution to the events of Boxing Day. There is usually an underlying reason for a big attitude. When you keep getting made out to be a bad guy when maybe you aren't so bad, well, they call that all kinds of fancy stuff in the psychology circles. There are rules of cause and effect that impact how we behave based on the ways others expect us to behave. Something related to the power of expectations and the inherent emotional experiences of self-loathing.

So, if police expect the worst from a guy, chances are that they are going to see it.

Self-fulfilling prophesy, it's usually called when the person becomes the person we expect them to be. Fiction, it's called, when so much isn't true.

Other than wanting to know which gun killed Jane Creba, police wanted to know if Big Guy was one of the shooters. They wouldn't be able to prove it, so the prosecutors changed their story at two separate trials. Did Big Guy shoot? Did he pass the gun to a kid named JoJay? Seems neither of the prosecution's theories is what actually happened, but that truth would be buried until long after the trials and appeals ended.

The wiretaps continued to provide some evidence. Just short of eighteen hundred phone taps were recorded and transcribed between February 28, when the first request to authorize wiretaps was made by the court, and June 22, just after the raids came down.

Those raids took place in the early hours of June 13, 2006. They were conducted in fourteen different locations, and twenty-five men were arrested that day; fifty-six men in total were arrested (not necessarily charged) in relation to the case, almost all of them young, black men. Nine black men and one white young offender were charged for homicide. Six of them had their charges dropped because police didn't believe they fired guns. Four of them still spent four years in jail waiting for that decision to be made. Of the five men finally charged with criminal code and drug charges, three of them became witnesses, one potential informant was killed on the streets (Eric Boateng), and one was acquitted.

But only one bullet killed Jane.

Two of the guys there that day (Richie and Boy) would be called to testify. Strange thing, given that Boy almost certainly had a gun and may have in fact been the one who shot Jovi in the leg. And yet, the bullet that wound up in Jovi's leg? Well, that one wasn't investigated.

Why was Boy never charged even though he was there that day and likely had a gun? How was it that his testimony in court said he wasn't even with Short that day? His claim that he wasn't the white guy standing beside Short that day seemed to go completely unchallenged, despite the fact that he wound up with that bullet in his leg. Why? How? Maybe because he wasn't the main target for the prosecution, and maybe because it was easier to testify that he was just shot than to go down with his brothers.

You couldn't blame Boy for doing this. He had family. He had to protect himself.

Some were arrested because the police had evidence that they were on Yonge Street on Boxing Day, but most of them were arrested primarily because they were thought to have some knowledge of the events and might be persuaded to testify.

Marz was one of those guys. Not because he was downtown. Why then?

Marz was brought in during the big sweep in June that hit all of the major projects — not for being involved in the Creba murder, but for trafficking. Stuck in jail before the preliminary hearing, the police tried to get him to come clean and break the code. They knew Marz knew what went down. Maybe they knew about the Crime Stoppers call. He certainly thought that was why he was arrested. Or maybe they just had him tied to Short's phone. Or Boy's.

When you live in a hood where distrust is breakfast, you're gonna wonder who poisoned your day. Was it cops or brothers?

During the interview after the raids, the police asked Marz, "How do you know Shackles?" His stomach sank. He didn't know that Boy had changed his phone contact details from Short to Shackles or that Short now went by the name of Shackles when he made the call to Visa to tell him not to rat. Marz thought he was the only one using the new moniker, and assumed the police had been tapping his phone.

It wasn't his phone that was tapped; it was Boy's. But Marz didn't know that.

Why would anyone "come clean" if it meant he would lose his home, family, friends, and city by becoming an informant in witness protection? Marz was sure that "someone" on the inside had already let people in the neighbourhood know that he made that Crime Stoppers call back in January. The call he thought was anonymous. The call he thought would stop more bloodshed. The call he thought was now making him a rat, even if he never admitted it to a soul. And it was the call that he thought would put everyone in his family in danger if he ever went back home. Marz didn't seem to have a choice. The guy who was nowhere near the Boxing Day shooting because he was at home. The investigators had successfully spooked him.

Marz eventually told. Jails are divided into "ranges" — divisions where the inmates within them will necessarily interact when they aren't in their cells. They moved Marz around to different ranges where he saw arch rivals who would stare him down. Tell him that even if he got out, word was already out on the street that he was a rat. Rats don't live long out of captivity. Rats put their family's lives at stake. Something Marz couldn't bear to see happen to his mother and other brother who was managing to keep himself on the right path away from the guns and drugs. So he had to make a decision fast. Get protection. Become a confidential informant. Be moved away from any contact with friends and family. And take on a different kind of life sentence far worse than a prison cell.

They gave him a week to decide.

No financial compensation. No secret deal for reduced charges.

Imagine you've got a week to decide if you want your family safe but to never see them again. You're told you won't have a history or be able to tell anyone about your history. You have no more contact with your parents or siblings or children or friends. Say goodbye to everything you've ever known.

Marz opted for the life sentence and relocation over the death sentence he was sure he and his younger brother would face back in the hood. He didn't want to be another statistic.

If you're a confidential informant in witness protection, any minor slip will take all of those rights to protection away. A relatively small misdemeanor eventually did so for Marz, but only after the he had sold his soul to the justice system and given them everything he knew. He's out of the province now, and still can't contact his family, but he no longer has the informant protection in place.

Some life sentences are just that.

No exclamation mark.

No jail time with three square meals.

And nobody bitching about how you've used the system because the system used you and most of society don't know it.

9

Courting Justice

Guns unaccompanied, sneakingly tiptoe across a
    porous border
With an obvious intent to make black youths much
    harder.

         — Lawrence Woodcock,
         "Give Youths a Chance"

Aesop told us very long ago: "Every truth has two sides. It is well to look at both before we commit ourselves to either." Justice isn't really about just two sides; if you want truth, you have to look well beyond two sides of any story.

Balancing prosecution and defence is our justice system. They're represented by the scales of justice held up by Justitia, the Roman Goddess of Justice. She is depicted wearing a blindfold to show that the court will hear stories objectively, without fear or favour, regardless of wealth, power, or identity (including skin colour). In her left hand, the figure holds a sword facing downwards to represent punishment, but that sword is held below the scales so that punishment is not meted out until both truths and lies have been heard.

Vengeance is not meted out without careful deliberation, without listening, without logic. And when we move back up to the scales, those have to weigh society, safety, and criminal rehabilitation in order to ensure that when the sentence is served, society is safe. Not just vengeance.

Unfortunately, when we live in countries where the names of accused are published, many of us will jump to the conclusion that someone is guilty as soon as they are arrested, and that the defence lawyers are just looking for loopholes, as opposed to presenting another side of the story. In fact, stories abound of charges being dropped after investigation, but by then, a serious amount of damage has been done to the accused. Worse, there are innumerable cases where people have done time without doing the crime: David Milgaard, Steven Truscott, the Memphis Three. Those cases are famous, but we hear far less about the cases where charges get dropped because of an "oops," even if the lives of the accused have been completely changed by the mistake.

Case in point, in 2011 a Sault Ste. Marie (Ontario) newspaper published a story about a man charged with possession and distribution of child pornography.[1] A full year later those charges were dropped when the police realized that someone else had hacked into his system.[2] No, he didn't serve time in prison. Instead, he served a different kind of time. His life was ruined by the mere accusation.

Our media can destroy lives because our system allows names to be published after charges are laid, without trial, let alone a guilty verdict. Our detention system is the same for anyone convicted as it is for someone just charged. Often deplorable and dangerous conditions, with little or no access to services, including social workers or psychologists or counsellors.

So you sit in a cell waiting. Waiting for clarity on the accusations. Waiting for a trial. Waiting to see family and friends. Imagining how your life has changed by a mere accusation.

And if you're poor? Capable and effective legal assistance is difficult to get. So you sit waiting for that.

Ei incumbit probatio qui dicit, non qui negat. "The burden of proof is on he who declares not on he who denies." The presumption of innocence is not well understood. It is a fundamental right internationally. In the West, we'll rise publicly to say systems where people are incarcerated and tortured without charges are an abomination compared to our own. Turns out it's easy to point at people, to point at other cultures, but way harder to point at ourselves.

The first trial in the Jane Creba murder that would convict a young man was that of JoJay. He was a young offender, so the early reports and bans ensured he could only be called JSR by the media.

And even though JoJay was a young offender in a highly publicized trial where it would be virtually impossible to get a jury that could be objective in the case of a bunch of black guys killing a white girl, the Crown pushed hard for a jury trial. A judge-only trial would ensure that, at the very least, the law would be interpreted and applied correctly. A jury of people who had all been shocked by the Boxing Day shooting would have strong feelings about the young shooter in this brazen event.

The deputy attorney general pushed hard for a trial by jury, which was his right under the Youth Criminal Justice

Act. But Gary Grill, JoJay's lawyer, argued that it wasn't constitutional — JoJay had the right to:

A fair trial
To make full answer in defence
And to a trial within a reasonable time.

JoJay wasn't going to have the benefit of a fair trial within a reasonable time; the jury trial would be neither fair, nor timely. As Gill argued in court:

All of [his rights] have been violated. Constitutional rights trump whatever power the Deputy Attorney General's power conferred by an act of Parliament. The Charter is still the highest law of this land. Your Honour definitely has the power to grant such a remedy.[3]

The argument failed. The trial went to jury.

After the preliminary hearings where the court reviews the evidence to determine if the case should go to trial, the judge raised serious concerns that the Crown was not adequately disclosing its position.

It's something the law calls "abuse of process."

In fact, in 1999, a criminal justice review committee submitted something called "The Martin Committee Report," which concluded, after substantial research and input from various members of the general public and legal experts, that the rights of the accused needed to be protected while efficiencies were increased in the system. Key amongst its recommendations was the need for both defence counsel and prosecution to be overtly clear about their submissions to court. The judge at JoJay's trial cited this when he reprimanded the prosecution:

> That's why the Martin Report refers to the importance of holding people [in this case, the prosecution] to their admissions. That's why the pre-trial rules now require that if someone changes their position, they have to give notice to the other side. Why? To avoid the very situation we are in right now. Six weeks into a trial and the whole trial is going off the rails because someone's decided to change their position and didn't tell anybody.[4]

And because the prosecution was changing its theory about who the shooter was without telling either the court or the defence, this meant a longer delay to deal with the legal matters of process, which a jury would be excused from hearing.

The judge further reprimanded them for causing the significant delay with their change in position because of the timelines they would now face: "I ... question whether anyone necessarily wants a jury deliberating on a second degree murder charge of this type three days before Christmas."[5]

But the prosecution decided, as they moved forward with JoJay's trial, that despite the fact that there was no DNA on the trigger of the smoking gun JoJay was found holding, he was the one who fired Big Guy's gun.

The prosecution did agree that Short shot first, but according to JoJay, Short wasn't shooting at him. As he explained it: "Cause he [Short] knows whatever I would — he knows personally I was tryin'. I was callin' the white boy like stuff like, you know what I'm saying, tryin' to stop this shit — the little fight."[6] JoJay indeed wanted the fight that happened in the Eaton Centre to stop right there. He had told his pals to knock off the nonsense.

JoJay told the police that Big Guy just handed him the gun after the shooting. But that didn't make a lot of sense when the two weren't very close and Big Guy surely wouldn't have thought that JoJay would take the rap for him. The police pushed this in their initial interrogation:

> Detective Pitts: You described him as an acquaintance, right. That's your word not mine…. But you're the guy he gave the gun to. A gun that potentially, you know, could put him in jail for a number of years. Maybe not knowing that at the moment — well actually — yeah, at that moment he could have known, even if no one was killed, coulda gone to jail for a while.
>
> Simpson-Rowe: He probably thinks that "Oh, if I get caught I'll go down for him," probably.[7]

Pretty unlikely to think that an acquaintance would do time for murder. Pretty unlikely even that a best friend from the hood would take the fall.

How did JoJay know about this gun? Because Big Guy had previously been showing people the "baby," saying he stole it.

The police asked JoJay how Big Guy got the gun. He explained, "Just say he robbed him. He- he- he axed him to see it. The guy trusted him. He axed him to see it.... And never gave it back.... This guy that used to hang in Martha.... This guy named Tutu."[8]

The first of the trials over, the jury found JoJay guilty of second-degree murder. He got a life sentence with no chance of parole for seven years. Something his troubled adolescent mind would never have anticipated when he went downtown on Boxing Day. Something his troubled past and many challenges couldn't possibly prepare him to meet.

He had words for the court and jury that weren't polite.

Next up for a full trial were Tyshaun and Big Guy. And, despite the Crown maintaining the position that JoJay was the one who fired the gun during his trial, their position now changed. Big Guy fired and gave it to JoJay. New trial. New judge. New jury.

The judge at Big Guy and Tyshaun's combined trial had the same problem as the judge at JoJay's — the prosecution changing its story. Not that the public would ever hear this. The jury didn't even hear this. All of the discussion of the contradiction happened with the jury excused. That's what happens in court. There's a legal challenge that the jury can't hear because it might possibly bias their findings.

Perhaps the jury should have heard that the Crown changed its position on what went down. That information might have changed the jury's position on justice. No. You can't change your argument, the judge says to the prosecution. But they do. Trial One: JoJay shot the gun. Trial Two: Um, we meant Big Guy shot.

When JoJay returned to court as a witness for the Crown at Big Guy and Tyshaun's combined trial, he still had words, but wouldn't say much. He just said neither Tyshaun nor Big Guy were guilty of anything. He was scowling, uncooperative, and scary. After all, Short had already pleaded guilty and JoJay was serving a life sentence. It didn't make sense to him that more men should be found guilty for Jane's death when it was the one bullet that killed her.

The jury would only see an angry young man. They wouldn't hear why he was so angry.

It was a brilliant move by the Crown to have JoJay show up as a witness — paint Tyshaun and Big Guy with the same big, scary, gangsta brush. The one that would suggest all of these guys were liars. The jury was instructed to ignore JoJay's statements and attitude, but that would be akin to telling a group of people to "not think about an elephant," and then expect them not to.

After his outburst, the jury was asked to leave while JoJay was told that if he continued to be a "hostile witness," that if he said anything more, he would be found in contempt of court and he would end up serving more time. The jury returned to hear these words:

> Ladies and Gentlemen of the jury — Mr. Simpson-Rowe has never previously said [Big Guy] and [Tyshaun] are innocent. Nor has he previously said that they were not present outside the Footlocker on Dec 26, 2005. Accordingly, his evidence has no value and can you please ignore it.[9]

As he was instructed, JoJay said nothing more. He was cuffed and taken away.

Boy showed up to testify as well.

He got shot that day. Nobody asked if the reason he got shot was because he had a gun. Nobody ever questioned who shot him.

Boy just identified Big Guy and Tyshaun as being there and being shooters that day. Seemed a good thing to point at others to keep himself out of jail. The jurors would never hear of Marz's testimony that he was almost 100 percent sure that Boy was carrying a gun that day.

Richie Steele had to testify as well. He didn't appreciate it and had words for the court when he was brought in for the preliminary hearing. "I hope you are happy. You just killed me. That is what you did," Steele yelled at Justice Ian Nordheimer in the preliminary hearing. "This is justice at its best."

Steele swore at the Crown attorney as well, while his mother, Valerie Steele, called out, "Richard, stop it. Don't lose your cool," from the public gallery. When asked if he knew Tyshaun, Steele merely said "saw him once or twice." Of course, the jury wouldn't hear that this was a lie, even though the police knew it was because of a wiretap they had. The jury wouldn't hear that a wiretap between Richie and an unknown male in custody on March 7, 2006, had the male asking if Richie wanted him to "bank up" Tyshaun, who was there in custody on a mischief charge. Richie's response: "please." And, of course, they wouldn't know about the run-in the night before Boxing Day.

Then there was another witness with a sketchy story.

At Big Guy's trial, when asked about the gun, Kory said he couldn't remember what he had said at the preliminary hearing. So the Crown asked him to read a quote from the transcript of the hearing. He just stared down at the page shown to him without saying anything unti it became evident — he was illiterate. The Crown then asked him if he could read; he just answered "yeah," and stared again blankly at the transcript in front of him. Turns out he wasn't the best of witnesses, but the jurors must have believed some of his implausible story.

Big Guy was mad at him on the night of the shooting. Was it because, as Kory told it, Big Guy didn't like the fact that Kory stayed home that day? Or was it because, as Big Guy tried to argue at one point, Kory actually sold his gun to JoJay a day or so before the shooting? That story wouldn't fly. Even if they were "roommates" at one point, the two had enough hate on for each other by the time of the trials that anything was possible.

One key fact that neither jurors nor the public present at the trial would ever hear is that Big Guy was pissed off with Kory because Kory had taken Big Guy's better gun that day and didn't answer the phone when Big Guy called for it.

Kory had, in fact, been out earlier in the day with Tyshaun and his cousin, Dorian Wallace. They were at a Dufferin Street and Lawrence Avenue shopping mall not far from the Black Creek and Jungle areas called Lawrence Square. Not only was Kory there, he was bragging about having Big Guy's other gun on him. The guys went together to another mall, Yorkdale, an upscale mall right next to the Jungle. It was there he left Tyshaun and headed downtown with a friend to an area called Kensington Market, where he was looking to buy shoes.

He just went home after that. He didn't know anything about the day's events.

According to Kory, about twenty minutes after he got home the evening of the shooting a bunch of guys showed up. Kory knew better than to mess with Big Guy. Smoking pot as much as Kory did makes a person a little on the lazy side when it comes to confrontations. Big Guy said Kory needed to leave.

The odd thing about Kory's testimonies is that the more time passed, the clearer his memory became about what happened that night. Not exactly what happens to most people, especially someone who smokes as much weed as Kory did. Seems his evolving grudge with Big Guy just kept ramping up after the initial arrests and well into the actual trials. By the time of the real trial, he had clearly rehearsed a testimony. Probably with some help during the witness preparation.

Kory actually liked Tyshaun — thought of him as almost an older brother, someone he told police initially in his early interviews "would give the shirt off his back." Tyshaun often gave Kory money to catch a bus to go to school. All of Kory's early testimonies indicated a genuine respect and gratitude. By the time he reached preliminary trials, he was a little less kind to Tyshaun. And by the time he faced the actual trial in front of a jury, his version of events had changed significantly. Early on, he couldn't remember; by the time of the trial, he had a full narrative.

According to Kory at the trial, Big Guy repeatedly said, "I hope I didn't hit no one," and Tyshaun said he "fired off the whole clip," meaning that he had fired all the bullets in his gun. What Kory said Big Guy said may well have been true if Big Guy were trying to protect his reputation as the Big Guy. It's highly unlikely, though, that Tyshaun said he spent all of his bullets. That was far from the case.

The detectives had, by the time of the trial, figured out that his gun couldn't have fired more than once. The jury would never hear this. Instead, they heard that Tyshaun was there that day. They heard this summary of the first meeting with Tyshaun and the police after his arrest, first from Detective Gibson: "At the Eaton Centre there's video cameras everywhere. You can't walk through that place without being on camera like sixty times. It's crazy."

Yonge Street was the same. They further informed Tyshaun during his first interview that they knew he was there. As Detective Coulthard said, "Yeah, I think they say if you walk through downtown Toronto, you will be guaranteed like you go from Bloor to Queen Street, you're on video twenty, thirty times."

And then there were the cellphone towers. Once Tyshaun's phone records were tracked, the police knew exactly where he had been that day — a series of shopping malls — Lawrence Square, Yorkdale, then the Eaton Centre, then walking along Yonge Street. They knew exactly who he called despite the fact that his phone list certainly didn't resemble the names of the guys he was calling.

The interrogation continued on the first day of his arrest. Coulthard: "So here you're calling this guy, this guy, this guy, this guy and these guys, okay. Now we all know who these people really are, because these aren't the real names as you know.... It's not Derrick Johnson you're calling. It's not Era Costan and it's not Elizabeth Bolton."

The police didn't actually know that much about him despite their interrogation techniques that said they knew everything. None of those traces mattered.

What really busted him was a simple phone call he made

on Wednesday, April 19, 2006, at about 10:00 p.m. to a female friend. By then, his phone was tapped, so the police knew that he and his friend were talking about a male referred to as Adrian who had been showing off ever since he got a new car. Tyshaun advised his friend, Chemere, that he had done Adrian a lot of favours, including getting him a gun (referred to as a burner).

Apparently there had been an argument between him and Adrian, and Adrian had come looking for him. It may have been big talk, but it gave the police a lot of information about the gun used Boxing Day.

The cellphone tap went like this:

> Chemere: Isn't that the same burner you, isn't that the same burner you gave him?
> Tyshaun: Yeah, same one I gave him, yes sir.
> C: What the fuck, yeah.
> T: I dare him to come. That gun, yo, the joke with that gun. Broken, eh?
> C: It is?
> T: Yeah. After that, after that thing, whatever, after that thing happened?
> C: Yeah.
> T: It broke, B. Yo.
> C: And you sold it to him same way?
> T. Yeah. Sold it to him for two thousand dollars.
> C: Laughing
> T: Same way. He even asked me. He goes, "Sy, this gun is broken."

The conversation continued. He explained that the gun only fired one bullet before it locked up. That was indeed what had happened on Boxing Day.

It was the reason only a single 25-millimetre casing was found on the scene of the murder. The gun Tyshaun had fired. The real reason it only fired one shot that day was because the gun was cleaned with WD40 the week before. WD40 may be great for squeaky doors, but it's too thick an oil to work on a gun. The second bullet Tyshaun tried to fire got stuck in the chamber.

The two-thousand-dollar gun was junk because of a cheap lube job.

The jurors didn't hear any of this information that came out during the interrogation and investigation. They just heard and accepted the sketchy details from Kory that implicated both Tyshaun and Big Guy as shooters. This testimony from a guy who smoked a lot of dope. This guy who changed his story every time he was asked to tell it. This guy who was trying to keep himself out of jail because his prints were on the gun.

As the trials finished up, the jurors found both Tyshaun and Big Guy guilty of manslaughter. Both men and their families were relieved that it wasn't a second-degree murder conviction, as had been the case for both Short and JoJay.

The press didn't report that only one bullet killed Jane, and that two men had been convicted of second-degree mur-der already. Instead, it reported this:

> The Creba family say they are grateful that two men have been convicted of manslaugh-ter in the Boxing Day 2005 shooting of their daughter Jane.

"They are happy with the outcome," Det.-Sgt. Savas Kyriacou told reporters Thursday after a jury convicted Louis Raphael Woodcock, 23, and Tyshaun Barnett, 22.[10]

10

Swing Low

Swing low, sweet chariot
Coming for to carry me home
—Traditional Song

"Swing Low" was a traditional, spiritual song that conveyed a secret message to slaves about how to escape slavery and get to Canada. Many spirituals had the intent of conveying a message of escape. Here's the thing: slavery can last well beyond that sole proprietorship of a man owning a man; persecution lasts well beyond generations of ownership.

We'd like to believe many refugees escaped persecution by coming to Canada. We'd like to believe everyone has "come home" to a place of acceptance.

Two of the four convicted for Jane's death would file appeals. JoJay and Big Guy.

When JoJay's appeal finally came forward, the appellate court agreed that his constitutional rights had *not* been violated, and that he had deserved to be tried as an adult with a jury despite the fact that it was a highly politicized case involving race and a youth. His appeal was dismissed in the same way that society had dismissed this young, messed-up man.

The media reports about JoJay's appeal received an abundance of responses reflecting the same sentiments as when he was first sentenced. After the *National Post* report on the appeal, comments posted by the sort of people who post anonymously came in a flurry. They suggested he be caged for life, castrated, hanged because he didn't deserve to have electricity wasted on him, and that his parents should also be jailed for life. More than a few sentiments suggested he be shipped "back" to Jamaica, even if he was born in Canada.

How does a kid grow up to be that hated? Or his parents?

Tyshaun did not appeal his conviction. Big Guy's appeal went along quietly and nothing changed in the end for him, despite the fact that during JoJay's appeal the Crown actually said, "You can exclude Louis Woodcock as a shooter."

He wasn't a shooter.

Would the public care? Would the law care?

The appeal court couldn't hear the part of the story where the prosecution actually admitted that he didn't shoot. Appeal courts can only hear whether the law was applied.

The media only reported that his appeal failed. They couldn't possibly report on the context of that conflict of information. The public wouldn't care.

The public also never heard about some of the poor treatment Big Guy faced in prison. They didn't hear about his parents travelling from Toronto to Kingston to visit him and his mother being turned away. A woman who doesn't even drink a full glass of wine, the officials said she had cocaine and heroin residue on her.

The public didn't hear that just before Big Guy was to be released, he was relocated to another prison in the middle of the winter without his clothes, and then put in solitary confinement. The guards alleged he had pot in his cell — certainly not something anyone who was to be released in just a few days would ever risk. Racism is even tougher inside these institutions than on the street. In jails, there isn't any sort of a trial to determine guilt. It's assumed without being proven. Stories of such don't make it to the media.

From the public's perspective, these guys were all just thugs. When you sell news, the deeper stories don't matter, the lives of thugs don't matter. Big Guy was there and he had a gun. Forget that he was too scared to actually fire it.

His life was one of many that didn't really matter.

Eric Boateng, GaYves Gandwimbi, and Anthony Moodie weren't that important. Their deaths never really made it to the news beyond a simple report of a homicide.

In fact, Anthony's murder was written off as a self-inflicted accident, even though a gun was never found and the witness statements were pretty sketchy. Not sure how someone who apparently accidentally shot himself could have hidden his gun. But it went without any further investigation, despite Anthony's father's pleas for justice to be done.

Eric was the seventieth murder victim of 2007. Even if 2005 was touted as the Year of the Gun, with seventy-eight murder investigations culminating in Jane Creba's in December, it seems 2007 was actually a busier year. Jane was the seventieth shooting victim in 2005; Eric was the seventieth homicide in 2007, with two months still left in that year. Eric's violent daytime murder that took place right near the Don Jail after his "call down" to visit someone. Police reported they were looking for "a guy in baggy pants and a black hat."[1] Hardly the same police hunt that Jane Creba had. They never found Eric's killer. Go figure.

Another person suspected of being a shooter on the day of the Jane Creba murder, Jermaine (J9) Osbourne, was killed in a brazen daytime shooting on June 6, 2006, just before the major busts, as he was just walking downtown, near St. Lawrence Market. He wouldn't live to be charged with anything. The police charged Creedy with his murder, but those charges were eventually dropped. Why the Crown decided not to proceed with a trial is a question that was never brought up in the media. And why it was dropped as a cold case is just a clear question of whose lives and deaths matter.

These men didn't have Kyriacou and more than a hundred police officers looking for their murderers. These men didn't have a city up in arms over their deaths.

Some of the men there that day lived and they are rebuilding their lives. Others are stuck.

Short is one who's stuck. He's alive and well, but being hustled from one prison to another as he continues to get himself into trouble. At last contact, he claimed that the lawyers are the real criminals and that people like him keep them, the courts, and the police, employed. He is looking forward to writing a book about his life. He seems to still have quite a distorted view. He seems to think anyone publicly employed is employed by him; a common concern amongst taxpayers even when they don't pay much in the way of taxes.

In 2010, Richie Steele was convicted of possessing a loaded semi-automatic pistol that was partially hidden under the passenger seat of his mother's car. He served the equivalent of his six-and-a-half-year sentence. His mother remains a strong community activist despite her fears that some young men are targeted because of their parents' attempts to work against racism. Richie has a strong role model in his mother. As he gets older, he may come to realize that he needs to take his fights to the social level rather than the streets.

Big Guy was released to a halfway house and is working hard to regain his life. His family prays every day that he has found the path out of his violent history. It seems that since word got out that he froze on Yonge Street that day, he won't be seen as the same Big Guy. It might be time to become Good Guy. His father continues to celebrate visual art and poetry through their church and selling his paintings and hopes his son will return to find the same passion and desire to serve as well as stay clear of the law.

Marz is living outside of the province, pursuing a job in the trades and keeping his nose clean. He misses his family and friends in Toronto, but he also knows it isn't safe for him to return. After a reporter put his name and information "out there," he hit rock bottom in 2008 and tried to commit suicide. He has his wits about him now and thinks back on what worked and didn't work in the system.

As he tells it, the thirteen to seventeen age range for young men is a "teeter-totter" time. When he was that age, Bob Rae was the Ontario premier (with the governing New Democrat Party — as socialist as Canada offers in its major political parties) who had put into place a program called JOY (Jobs Ontario Youth) that guaranteed the young men work. Marz said, "God bless him," for that. At that time, a kid could go to the career centre and look in a large, black binder to find careers listed by A to Z. The kids were then paid to go to the Toronto Industrial School of Trades and provided bus fare and supplies. One of the first big rappers hailing from Toronto benefitted from another JOY program.

Kardinal Offishall was the first Canadian rapper to break into the Hot 100 in 2008 with a song called "Dangerous." Offishall was able to take the Fresh Arts program, and cites it as being a significant foundation for his success.

But the New Democrats were replaced by an ultra-conservative majority in the province, and under the leadership of Mike Harris, all social programs were taken away leaving only welfare as a tentative option — and that relied on heavily policed systems that regulated who got money, how much they got, and what they had to prove each month to continue receiving it.

Stripping services clearly isn't the answer to supporting the "teeter-totter" young men who need support to make the right decisions. Breaking up communities also isn't the way, even though the new Regent Park plans will eventually help to "break up" the ghetto.

All the Toronto hip-hop artists who were interviewed for this book said the same thing: there needs to be more funding for the arts to build the confidence of the young boys and girls in the "ghettos," so that they are encouraged to believe they *can* achieve their dreams. When the Toronto media conglomerate CHUM (owned by one of the three major media corporations in Canada — Bell Media) took over the Flow Toronto urban radio station in 2010, local artists lost their voice on the radio. Large corporations are more interested in featuring mainstream artists who bring in the advertising money than they are in supporting local musicians.

All of the men who were charged but not convicted were aspiring artists. Instead of being given a place for their voice, they spent substantial time awaiting trial before being acquitted — forty-seven months each when they didn't even have guns that day. Almost four years in prison, just for being there on Boxing Day. And frankly, for being black.

When Dorian Wallace got out of the hospital he was deported back to England, as he had an expired travel visa and was thought to have just been a bystander. He was eventually arrested in London, England, and ordered to be extradited back to Canada in the summer of 2009. That never happened. It would have been pointless. He didn't have a gun that day either.

Tyshaun has been released to a halfway house where he is pursuing schooling in the trades. His mother and stepfather eagerly await his return home to a quiet and spacious country residence north of Barrie where work in the construction business awaits him through his stepfather's business. He has hopes of teaching young, black men that the gangsta lifestyle is not an answer to their struggles. His young son often spends time with grandma and the extended family. Tyshaun wants to come back from this tragedy with a mission to help young people.

Tyshaun's mother, Patricia, did not return to dancing after the assault that left her near dead. Instead of turning back to drugs, she turned herself once again to the one constant that she had as a child: her church. She began attending school to be a social-service worker and, eventually, an addictions counsellor. She had a life story to tell and a calling to help other young women turn their lives around so that they wouldn't face the tragedies she and her family had faced. Her only "drug of choice" now is the odd game of bingo.

As for some of the other guys who were affiliated with the shooters?

In April 2012, Christopher "Creedy" Lewis was sentenced to life imprisonment with no parole for twelve years for his involvement in the shooting death of Kerlon Charles.

Cleavon Springer, a reformed bad guy doing right, was an eyewitness to the murder. Like Marz's reaction to the Creba shooting, Cleavon decided that changes needed to happen in his neighbourhood, even if that meant he would become a "rat." After testifying at another murder trial — despite his own history of running drugs and guns, a kidnapping, a home invasion, and involvement in two murders — he showed others that it is possible to leave the life of a thug. Cleavon's testimony led to a life sentence for Creedy. Like Marz, Cleavon showed others that there was a way out of the cycle of violence.

As Cleavon told it, "Even if my story breaks down the invisible wall of silence for one person then I feel like it wasn't in vain. Us as black men have to take it upon ourselves to change; we can't look towards others to do it for us."

During both murder trials where Cleavon testified, he gave jurors a gritty and often disturbingly graphic account of the senseless violence that plays out on city streets. And he helped them to understand a little of the mentality of a thug. "We were desensitized," he testified. "We didn't have much empathy when it came to human beings, we just looked on them as a rival."

Springer is living his life now as a law-abiding man.

JoJay is still in prison. Early into his jailing, he had numerous psychological tests done that revealed both his

ADHD and a high potential to re-offend. Some of the tests also showed that he has psychopathic tendencies; however, the psychologists testing him also cautioned that he was only twenty years old when the tests were conducted, and that a personality assessment could not be fully done until the mid-twenties, which is when a young person's personality has matured enough (i.e., is capable or relying on their frontal cortex).

As Justice Nordheimmer declared at JoJay's sentencing, while a lack of parenting undoubtedly had an impact on his life choices, he was still culpable:

> Mr. Simpson-Rowe's character flaws are, to a degree, understandable given his background. I do not intend to repeat all of the detail in regard from the assessment report. It is sufficient by way of summary to say that Mr. Simpson-Rowe's upbringing, especially his lack of proper parental involvement and supervision, undoubtedly led him to where he is today.
>
> The legitimate frustration that any outside observer would feel at this often repeating scenario of parental omission giving rise to adolescent criminal activity does not change the fact that the court must deal with Mr. Simpson-Rowe as he is, not as we would have wished him to be.
>
> The realities of Mr. Simpson-Rowe's background may explain his current situation but they do not absolve him of all personal

responsibility for his acts; nor do they alter the reality that Mr. Simpson-Rowe poses a clear challenge in terms of any prospect for his rehabilitation and reintegration into society. His record, his other encounters with the police, his anger management and related problems and the test results from the assessment, all point to a likelihood of his committing further offences in the future.

I have concluded that an adult sentence is necessary in this case. I believe that a youth sentence would fail to address the seriousness of the offence and Mr. Simpson-Rowe's role in it. It would fail to hold Mr. Simpson-Rowe accountable for what he chose to do.[2]

JoJay has continued to struggle. He was denied parole in July 2015. According to his parole board hearing, he wasn't ready to go. The parole board accepted that he had a troubled past, but couldn't support a position that said that he would not have a troubled future. So, as much as some people want to believe these guys get off "scott free," that's not usually the case.

The board noted Simpson-Rowe's past involved a "dysfunctional childhood" and physical abuse. "You have a history of associating with individuals who are involved in criminal activity and have traditionally looked up to older, criminally entrenched peers for support and a sense of family," the board's decision said. In his hearing, it was reported that he continued to have problems interacting with his peers and respecting authority.

As much as we may loathe this violent behaviour and want to lock it away, one has to wonder if any child would choose such an existence. To choose parents who aren't there to give their support. Or to choose race. Or to choose poverty. Or to choose to be hated. At what age is that choice made? And how do we fix that attitude so that JoJay can eventually come out of prison and be a safe, contributing citizen?

EPILOGUE

Move Mountains

I was made to move mountains
I was born to be astounding
I was grown with a good heart
The type to dive in the water — deal with the sharks
Whoever survived yo' we threw them on the Arc
No i ain't Noah and no i ain't Jesus
Just a man that grew up
Two brothers in the co-op

— Choclair, "Made"

People don't think of colour when they're white, but they do think about it a lot when they aren't. Written back in 1989, here are a few of the fifty privileges that white people take for granted, as outlined by Dr. Peggy McIntosh:

2. I can avoid spending time with people whom I was trained to mistrust and who have learned to mistrust my kind or me.

5. I can go shopping alone most of the time,

pretty well assured that I will not be followed or harassed.

6. I can turn on the television or open to the front page of the paper and see people of my race widely represented.

7. When I am told about our national heritage or about "civilization," I am shown that people of my color made it what it is.

8. I can be sure that my children will be given curricular materials that testify to the existence of their race.

9. If I want to, I can be pretty sure of finding a publisher for this piece on white privilege.[1]

So what distinguishes "us" from "them"? Black from white? Impoverished from middle class? A lot. Mostly, it's how we wake up each day, how we go about our day, what we think about, how we act, how we finish our day. Hell. That's our whole day. Ultimately, the art any one person produces is a reflection of their day.

Hip hop and rap are reflections of the daily life and struggles of the artists who create within that form, just as the songs of Bruce Springsteen represent the world he grew up in. Working class.

All of the guys associated with Jane Creba's murder were simply people trying to escape their lives. There were three main escapes: friendship, drugs, and music.

So what killed Jane? Easy.

It was the bullet fired by Jeremiah "Short" Valentine's .357 Magnum.

What really killed Jane? What killed Eric Boateng, Jermaine Osbourne, Anthony Moodie, Walter Scott, Freddie Gray? What sent Marz to a new place to live without any connection to family or friends? What continues to cause violent riots to the south of Canada and quiet riots here? Frustration, poverty, fear....

One word: Racism. Or four words: People who aren't white. Another four words have cropped up lately too: Don't let them in. The main threat that is being voiced here is "difference," but the bigger threat is "deference" — a passivity that prevents us from asking questions.

We can call them terrorists because they are brown. We can call them thugs because they are dark brown. We can always say that they are "other," because they are broken and somehow we have forgotten that most of the white colonizers of the world came to their places in new lands because they were broken. Potato famines. Poor conditions to grow crops. Wars.

But most immigrants (or our parents, or grandparents, or great grandparents) *chose* to come to new countries. They weren't forced to.

Consider that the ancestors of many African Canadians and African Americans came to our countries as broken families to begin with. Men were captured and taken from their homes, brought here against their will. If we think that's just history and everyone needs to get over it, well, that's just another oversimplification of a cultural tragedy.

Similarly, when Canada sent Aboriginal children far from their families to "convert" them out of their cultural ways in residential schools, our government caused scarring that is seemingly impossible to mend. This has led to addiction, suicide, violence, rapes, and the continued abuse of Aboriginal women.

In the U.S., black men are six times more likely to be imprisoned than non-blacks. Currently, there are more black men in prison than there were slaves prior to the abolition of slavery. In Canada, we tend to have the same problem with our Aboriginal population for the exact same reasons. Decades of poverty, social systems that give a second-class-citizen status that would allow for thousands of missing and murdered Aboriginal women who "fell through the cracks."

There are still people who blatantly refer to the non-whites as animals — do a Google search for "black men are lazy"; do a search for "blacks are animals." They present those statements as facts rather than racism. "They're the ones using the system. Welfare and all that." "People of colour just don't work as hard. They want it given to them." Fox News in the U.S. quite openly reports that young black men are "raised without structure" so they "often reject the education structure and gravitate towards vice." Racism is a strong force, established and upheld by social systems, institutions, and policy.

We'd like to think the civil rights movement created equality for all long ago, but that hasn't been the case; the effects of institutional racism remain. Between 1934 and 1962 the U.S. government handed out billions of dollars in home loans. But those weren't available to anyone black, a system eventually referred to as *redlining*, which would ensure that only whites could get out of poverty and find ways to wealth. In the U.S., that's what caused the development of ghettos.

People of colour were not able to invest in housing that could then be passed on down through generations, forming the sort of wealth that many white people have. This largely impacts the quality of education available to those who are impoverished when segregation — though not a law — is definitely a part of our system's fabric.[2]

And if we think that's just a historical hiccup, let's not kid ourselves. Insurance companies, banks, and credit card companies still deny services to people living in inner city "problem areas," or charge them more than their counterparts in more affluent areas. Environmental racism still exists as well when children have inferior conditions in which to play (such as a "park where we don't play") and are faced by decay in public works and housing. In cities where liquor is sold privately (unlike in Ontario), there are also more liquor stores in impoverished areas, contributing to further problems with addiction as well as violence and theft.

There are persistent ideas, held by some, that anyone on welfare is an abuser of systems, or that anyone charged is automatically guilty, or has some defence lawyer making a joke out of our justice system using taxpayers' money. There are sentiments that we need to stop letting immigrants into our country because they abuse our systems. Or sentiments that say the Aboriginal peoples have already had too much support; that they are *not* entitled to more, because they can't seem to manage their own affairs.

There is a theory that some educators in the realm of social justice call "racial nihilism." That is to say that, while we may argue that race is a political, social, and cultural construct, and not a "reality" of human differences at some sort of biological level, we cannot claim that racial distinctions (and ultimately racism) exist at some fundamental level in our perspectives. This theory is most prominent when people say "I don't see colour" when referring to interactions with other people.

In 2015 the Toronto Police allegedly put a hold on the practice of "carding" — where anyone can be stopped by police and asked for I.D. and to report their activities. The media would tell us just how rampant this practice had become.

> Police carded people more than 2 million times between 2008 and 2013. That's according to police reports obtained by the *Toronto Star* under a freedom of information request. The statistics show that visible minorities, especially African-Canadians, were significantly more likely to be stopped and carded. In about 450,000 of those cases, the person carded was African-Canadian ... and that's in a city with 200,000 African-Canadians living it."[3]

Newly appointed African-Canadian police chief Mark Saunders has defended carding, even while he admitted that he was "interrogated" on the streets using this method when he was a teen. Many activists, and even the justice minister of Ontario, have called carding an unconstitutional act that creates barriers instead of forging relationships that would enhance community safety.

The relatively newly appointed Ontario provincial government, as well as the federal government, have made a point that they want our systems to change. End carding.

End the "tough on crime" legislation that was brought in by the previous Canadian government.

Oddly enough, some blacks sided with the police chief. They differentiate between the civil and the uncivilized, arguing that the uncivil don't deserve "free" civil rights. American author Taleeb Starkes wrote a controversial book on the differentiation of "blacks" and "niggers" that mirrored such sentiments, titled *The Un-Civil War: Blacks vs. Niggers: Confronting the Subculture within the African American Community:*

> Ironically, NIGGERS will zealously jump for anything that's free, except education. They're unconcerned with the history regarding this "free" public school education, which in actuality, wasn't obtained freely. In fact, while being physically assaulted, pelted with rocks, bitten by dogs, sprayed with fire hoses, and indiscriminately arrested, a racially diverse citizenry paid for these "rights" through blood, sweat, and tears. Nevertheless, the NIGGER subculture expects to enjoy these "rights" without accepting any of the attached responsibilities. Those who don't care that "rights" are accompanied with responsibility should be denied those rights. In other words, Civil Rights shouldn't be extended to those intentionally, lacking civility. Ironically, in the not too distant past, African-Americans had to be escorted "to" schools; presently, JuviNIGGERS are being escorted "from" schools. Go figure.[4]

With all due respect to a fellow author, Starkes just sold out brothers to a neo-conservative ideology that would have us separate people into "us versus them." An easy dichotomy. Take people down by making them feel isolated and unwanted. Starkes's message — there are "Niggers" and there are "the righteous" ones — ain't helping anyone but the people who keep other people down.

Shout out to change, not to propagate.

Virtually all of the men who participated in the Boxing Day shootout had been escorted out of their schools for various reasons — not necessarily because they took education for granted. The development of an Africentric elementary school in one Toronto area near Jane and Finch — with curriculum that celebrates black history, artists, authors, scientists, and leaders — has certainly proven to be a strong support mechanism for students that results in greater self-confidence, cultural pride, and enhanced critical thinking.[5] Better schools and programs where self-confidence comes before any other form of education are one answer, but they certainly can't be the only answer.

If you don't feel you have the protection of family, it's human nature to seek comfort in large groups and/or to choose some sort of drugs to ease the pain. There's still a choice to make. Clearly, you can choose not to be a thug ... but it's a lot tougher for the young men in these projects to make good choices than it is for a middle-class person who chooses not to break the law.

While efforts to revitalize Regent Park are still underway, the changes that have occurred have caused problems. The grudges that were once only held in that hood are now being spread out through the city, as the low-income/socially assisted families get shuffled around into other low-income neighbourhoods. As much as the revitalization appears, from the outside, to be a genuine effort to help, in some ways it has become another way to displace the already displaced.

More efforts are needed to ensure communities are genuinely supported, and that the people within those communities feel safe and prepared to support each other. These efforts need to be especially focused on helping the young men struggling to find an identity.

Creative outlets are one choice for avoiding addiction and finding a group of engaged peers. Rap is a great option, but not when the point of it is to promote and celebrate violence and the hyper-sexualizing and belittling of women.

The hip-hop artists who are "real" are about teaching young people to have confidence in themselves. Frankie Payne, a rapper from near the Black Creek area regularly hosts fundraisers alongside other MCs, and makes sure the proceeds make it back to the children in the community. He wants the kids to believe in themselves and believe they can overcome the challenges of being black and poor. Toronto artist Dan-e-o regularly works in community centres, in housing projects, and for various organizations and schools to teach young people the real art of hip hop. He teaches them first and foremost to have confidence in themselves and to feel proud of their own creativity. However, such efforts are few and far between in the grand scheme of things. As Dan-e-o tells it, these programs can only be as good as the outreach in place, and that requires education, communication, and funding. The arts need to be promoted by federal, provincial, and local governments and the programs have to be rooted in the neighbourhoods and their needs.

Despite having his picture taken within the "hoods" with his "brothers," former mayor Rob Ford had no interest in supporting the arts and the cultural needs of these communities. The federal ultra-conservative government that introduced so many prison bills and reduced funding to the arts obviously did not support such communities. And even though the orthodox right lost in the 2015 federal election, it will take years to bring back social policies and programs and to undo the damage of the previous government's "tough on crime" legislation.

There are other musical options as well. Gospel music still provides a sense of community and purpose.

Orim Meikle, an Alabama pastor who oversees a church right next to Downview Airport, not far from the Jane-Finch area, has thoughts on how to help. He is the senior pastor with Rhema Christian Ministries, one of Toronto's fastest growing churches. He preaches at the funerals of young black men gunned down on the streets. He tells the guys like JoJay, Big Guy, Short, and the rest of the young men drawn to violence to put down their guns and stop impregnating women. He tells the young women that God wants them to be more than baby mamas living in poverty in areas like Regent Park and Jane-Finch and the Jungle and Black Creek and many socially assisted housing areas in the east end of the city. He preaches to an ever-expanding "vibrant church" of thousands of parishioners that using the reality of racism as an excuse for immorality is just that — an excuse for shirking responsibility. He sets the stage for change by offering parents courses on parenting and money management, and young people music and choir programs to shift them away from the gangsta rap that seems to take over their lives. He runs a Sunday school, and has dreams of eventually opening elementary and secondary schools.

Spirituality has long been identified with black culture. Church has played a particularly important role in addressing various supportive needs in African-American (and, by extension, African-Canadian) communities in areas such as community organizing and support. When the Underground Railroad brought blacks to Canada, their churches, which had been so important to them before they fled the south, were soon transplanted here. The church has historically presented African Canadians with a sense of worth, ultimately necessary if people were to deal with racism. If, throughout the week, people met with various forms of systemic racism in their workplaces, schools, and broader society, Sunday gave back a sense of pride and dignity, and ultimately hope, alongside people who had shared experiences.

The church today still avails that.

As researcher Gillian Wells has written, based on her personal experience, the church continues to provide a sense of community, even if the focus has changed somewhat in the years since the civil rights movement:

> My father, an immigrant from the tiny Caribbean island of Grenada worked as a machinist during the day and brought home televisions to repair at night. But on Sundays he filled with pride as the treasurer of the church. As an immigrant, man, it gave him status, self-esteem, a position and role to fulfill that he did not have in mainstream society....
>
> As I look at the church today, it is now imperative for the church in this new climate to fight for the preservation of the Black

family, the Black youth and more specifically the Black male. It is a shift from an outward fight to an inward preservation.[6]

Without a sense of community, it is difficult to shine. It's one of the reasons hip-hop artists create a strong community if they are being true to the art form.

It's been ten years since the shooting of Jane Creba. Have any of the thugs learned any lessons? Has violence of this sort ended in Toronto?

In 2006, fifteen-year-old Jordan Manners was killed at his school in the Jane-Finch area. Two young men were acquitted when their testimonies kept changing. While it isn't quite clear what happened, Jordan may have been looking to buy a gun, which discharged accidentally in a school washroom.

In 2007, eleven-year-old Ephraim Brown was killed after being shot in the neck by a stray bullet just a few blocks south and between the Jane-Finch and Black Creek areas.

On June 2, 2012, in the food court of the Eaton Centre, five people were shot — one dying at the scene and one dying in hospital shortly after. It was gang rivalry according to all reports. The shooter, Christopher Husbands, had previously been stabbed thirty-five times in an apartment where he thought he was going to meet his on-and-off-again lover — a woman significantly older than him and also the mother of one of his friends. He was met instead by the assailants he would eventually shoot. Comparisons to the Creba shooting were immediate, because it was the same mall, and because it was black guys.

Just a month later, in July 2012, a family barbecue party was interrupted by what police described as "the worst act of gun violence in Toronto's history," which left fourteen-year-old Shyanne Charles and twenty-three-year-old Joshua Yasay murdered, and twenty-three others injured. Shaquan Mesquito, an eighteen-year-old from another project area of the city called Malvern, was found guilty of the murders and assaults. By all media accounts, it was a case of two gangs — the Galloway Boys versus the Malvern Boys.

We could believe what was reported and assume the incidents were just gangs fighting each other. Or we could ask questions. Chances are that there were many other stories intertwined in those events.

And yet, despite these tragic events, gun violence has actually been on the decline in Toronto for ten years. Is it because the federal government took a firm stand by increasing sentences? Not likely. Is it because fewer people are doing crack? Maybe. Is it because churches, schools, and community activists are doing a better job of providing support? That may be a factor.

Is it because "real" hip hop is getting its message out? Is it because some people of courage continue to want stories told and questions asked? We can hope so.

Is violence going away? Not any time soon.

Toronto saw an increase in the number of shootings in the summer of 2015. The media began calling it the Summer of the Gun, reflecting back ten years on the Year of the Gun. That spike in gun violence saw many young people killed in their communities — including a fourteen-year-old girl, Lecent Ross, who was just playing at a neighbour's house when she was shot by a thirteen-year-old boy who had gotten a hold of an eighteen-year-old's gun. By the year's end, twenty-seven people were murdered by guns in Toronto. Not great, by any means, but far less than in the Year of the Gun, which Toronto media were invoking in the face of the violence.

The Conservatives (reflecting the Republicans in the U.S. and other right-wing perspectives around the world) who ruled in Canada at the time wanted to see more jails built, more life sentences, a reduction of services available to those in prison, and a reduction of parole opportunities. In essence, their version of justice favoured the sword over the scale. Fortunately, they are no longer in power. People in Canada have returned to their roots of empathy. Pendulums do swing.

Some good things come of tragedies when there is an opportunity to reflect.

In the case of Ephraim's murder, the townhouse where the shooting occurred has been turned into a sort of club house for young people, with dancing lessons, cooking lessons, a homework club, and a computer lab being run by and for the community. After Jordan Manners's death , many schools now have community police officers that work there every day with the youth; they aren't there just to "police" or screen kids for guns — they are there to show the youth that not all police are "out to get them" ... that some police officers are a part of their community and trying to help.

Throughout North America, racism still runs rampant in our police services and our justice systems. Racial profiling continues to plague Toronto policing, just as much as it does to the south of us — granted, we are far more subtle about how we do it. We don't have cops shooting a guy eight times in the back as he's running away, and we don't have the riots of Baltimore. But we do have racism.

In May 2015, a man was awarded twenty-seven thousand dollars in a lawsuit against a police officer who punched him simply because he wouldn't take his hands out of his pocket during a carding incident. As of June 2015, there were three class-action law suits against the Toronto police being lead by the Black Action Defence Committee.

Not every cop is a racist, nor is every black guy a thug. But it is a fact that we continue to profile our African Canadians in a way that is controversial, whether in the media, in music, or via carding practices. There are many police officers working to bridge the gap between the haves and have-nots — many working within the communities themselves to support people. There are journalists who try to share various perspectives on race in the media. There are many hip-hop artists who speak of their trials and tribulations. These are the people who can communicate hope.

What killed Jane Creba is the same thing that kills anyone in an impoverished culture: a loss of hope.

But, as Dylan Thomas told his dying father in his poem (a villanelle) "Do Not Go Gentle into That Good Night," we all have a choice to make. "Rage, rage against the dying of the light." Rage not violently, but with the passion to find answers to very complex cultural problems. As a society, we all have to be passionate about recovering from the loss of our children to lives of violence. Ironically, a villanelle is a type of poetry that shares the same etymology as the word *villain*. Poets and thugs may come from the same place, and we can hope that the former will replace the latter, just as K'Naan showed us is possible.

And if we're going to fix anything, our first step is to stop pretending that racism is a thing of the past.

Rest in Peace, Jane.

Rest in Peace to all the people who died innocently in our many wars. Rest in Peace to all those who didn't die innocently.

T-dot-O.

As for those us that may carry our voices beyond the sewer grates on the street where Jane died … we have work to do … we have mountains to move.

ACKNOWLEDGEMENTS

have first and foremost to thank my children. They inspire me to write for the benefit of a better world as we face our fears and stand up to our bullies. Plus they tolerate the time I am too busy with writing to cook … and they still (mostly) laugh at my lame jokes.

Writing is a lonely sport. To my friends and colleagues who have grounded me in this work: I'm not mentioning your names because you wouldn't like that, so I'll make you cookies instead and hope you keep hanging out with me.

For the many artists and individuals who were willing to share their stories about their trials and tribulations: this book would not have been possible without your faith in me to bring your voices to the page.

I can't personally thank all of the people who work in so many different realms to better our society — to expose inequality, to support people with various needs that the broader society may not understand, to speak out, even if whispering is all you can do, to share culture, to question. Many of you work in areas this book has challenged: policing, social services, the courts, journalism, teaching, politics. I can only hope that this book has offered all of us ellipses. These. .... Dots. At the end of a sentence. An invitation to keep going.

For the many artists and individuals who were willing to share their stories about their trials and tribulations: this book would not have been possible without your faith in me to bring your voices and music to the page. These artists are part of a vibrant music community that is speaking to the very concerns raised in this book — they certainly deserve to have our attention.

And now to the last thank you. Writing isn't just about sitting down with pen to paper in a courtroom and fingers to a keyboard at my dining table. To my editor, Michael Melgaard, and to everyone at Dundurn Press: you are a remarkable team.

NOTES

Introduction

1. L. Diebel, "The Year of the Gun: Is this the end?" *Toronto Star*, December 31, 2005.

2. "Interactive: Toronto Homicides Since 1990," *Toronto Star*, http://www.thestar.com/news/crime/torontohomicidemap.html.

3. Linda Diebel, "Mother Works to Make Fighting Gun Violence National Priority," *Toronto Star*, September 6, 2013.

4. Ontario Human Rights Commission, *Paying the Price: The Human Cost of Racial Profiling*, 15.

Chapter 1

1. Juristat, Statistics Canada, select volumes 20–28.

2. *FBI Uniform Crime Reports.*

3. "Police Reported Crime Statistics," Statistics Canada, 2014.

Chapter 2

1. "Social Cohesion in Contested Space: A Neighbourhood Integration Framework for Regent Park." Final Report — December 2014, University of Toronto, Geography and Program in Planning Department, 5.

2. Ironically, Turk grew up in the north side of Regent, while Tyke grew up in the south.

3. Some members of Regent Park continue to argue that TnT is not a gang. See, for instance, "Eaton Centre shooting: Sic Thugs of Regent Park and the allure of gangs," *Toronto Star*, June 9, 2012.

Chapter 3

1. Steven Levitt and Stephen J. Dubner, *Freakonomics: A Rogue Economist Explores the Hidden Side of Everything* (Toronto: HarperCollins, 2009), chapter 3.

Chapter 4

1. "Why Are So Many Black Children in Foster and Group Homes?" *Toronto Star*, December 11, 2014.

Chapter 7

1. This quote comes from the first part of *The Waste Land*, "The Burial of the Dead." The working title for *The Waste Land* was "He Do the Police in Different Voices."

2. Peter Small, "Inside the Jane Creba murder investigation," *Toronto Star*, March 29, 2010.

3. Ibid.

4. Electronically recorded interview of Jorrell Simpson-Rowe by Detective Sergeant Sava Kyriacou (457) and Detective Sergeant Reg Pitts (765). (Statement, December 27, 2005, page 14.)

5. Electronically recorded interview of Jorrell Simpson-Rowe by Detective Sergeant Sava Kyriacou (457) and Detective Sergeant Reg Pitts (765). (Statement, January 1, 2006, page 251.)

6. Electronically recorded interview of Jorrell Simpson-Rowe by Detective Sergeant Sava Kyriacou (457) and Detective Sergeant Reg Pitts (765). (Statement, January 1, 2006, 1 vol 2, page 292.)

7. Electronically recorded interview of Jorrell Simpson-Rowe by Detective Sergeant Sava Kyriacou (457) and Detective Sergeant Reg Pitts (765). (Statement, January 2, 2006, page 72.)

Chapter 8

1. TnT/Sic Thugz would be implicated as a gang in two other homicides where raids almost replicated the Creba raids in May 2014, arresting almost fifty young, black men. Not a gang. But easier to report that way.

Chapter 9

1. "Sault Man, Youth Accused of Distributing Child Pornography," *SooToday.com*, April 6, 2011.

2. "Charged but not Convicted. What If It Was You?" *SooToday.com*, January 27, 2012.

3. JSR Trial Proceedings, volume 3, page 25–26.

4. JSR Trial Proceedings, volume 3, page 46.

5. JSR Trial Proceedings, volume 3, page 82.

6. Interview of Jorrell Simpson-Rowe by detectives, January 1, 2006, page 500.

7. Interview of Jorrell Simpson-Rowe by detectives, January 2, 2006, page 512.

8. Ibid., 518.

9. Thursday Feb 25, 2010, court transcripts.

10. Peter Small, "Manslaughter Convictions in Creba Shooting." *Toronto Star*, April 1, 2010.

Chapter 10

1. "Victim Gunned Down Outside Jail Was Charged During Jane Creba Shooting," *CityNews*, Oct 22, 2007, accessed April 12, 2016.

2. "Judge's Ruling in JSR Sentence Covers Wide Range of Issues," *CityNews*, April 24, 2009, accessed April 12, 2016.

Epilogue

1. Peggy McIntosh, "White Privilege: Unpacking the Invisible Knapsack," http://ted.coe.wayne.edu/ele3600/mcintosh.html.

2. For examples of the effects of redlining, see: Alexis C. Madrigal, "The Racist Housing Policy in your Neighborhood," *The Atlantic*, May 22, 2014, and, Emily Badger, "Redlining: Still a Thing," *Washington Post*, May 28, 2015.

3. Jim Rankin, "Carding Drops but Proportion of Blacks Stopped by Toronto Police Rises," *Toronto Star*, July 26, 2014.

4. Taleeb Starkes, *The Uncivil War: Blacks vs. Niggers: Confronting the Subculture within the African American Community* (Politically Incorrect Publishing, 2013).

5. "Africentric Alternative School Research Project: Year 3 (2013–14)," jointly undertaken by York University and Toronto District School Board, http://ycec.edu.yorku.ca/files/2012/11/AAS-Research-Project-Year-3-Report.pdf.

6. Gillian Wells, "The Answer Within — The Role of the Church in the Black Community: A Community Development Response to the Violence in Toronto," presented at the First North American Conference on Spirituality and Social Work, May 2006.

MORE FROM DUNDURN

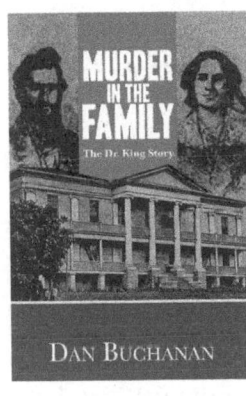

Murder in the Family
The Dr. King Story
Dan Buchanan

As the old saying goes, "You can pick your friends, but not your relatives." In tranquil Northumberland County, Ontario, two families are well acquainted with the grim truth of that innocuous-sounding expression. They are the descendants of the first, and only, man executed in Northumberland's history. In a sordid true-crime tale of poison and philandering in 1850s Ontario, the respected Dr. William Henry King astonished the countryside with the sinister murder of his wife and with his subsequent attempts to evade justice. His capture and conviction were triumphs of vengeful relatives and early forensic science.

Dan Buchanan, a blood relative of Dr. King's, grew up dogged by rumours of his ancestor's bloody crime, but family shame and obfuscation left him with more questions as time wore on. Now, based on original documents, breathless reportage of the sensational King trial, and interviews held just after the notorious hanging, Buchanan reconstructs the full tale of crime and punishment, which shocked the province and has engendered speculation for over a century and a half.

Through the Eyes of Serial Killers
Interviews with Seven Murderers
Nadia Fezzani

Journalist Nadia Fezzani spent years probing the minds of serial killers in search of answers to unsettling questions: What went on in their heads as they prepared for their next crime? What drove them to murder not once, but habitually? Were they born killers, or had they begun as normal individuals and been somehow transformed into predators?

Fezzani conducted groundbreaking, uncensored interviews with multiple-murderers behind bars. The account she pieces together from interviews, psychological research, criminal profiling, and genetic studies, is as unsettling as it is undeniable. The scars of abuse, and cold-blooded logic all emerge as Fezzani dissects serial killers' personalities in a quest to understand those who have committed unthinkable crimes.

Through the Eyes of Serial Killers explores the leading theories on the psychology of serial killing, victim selection, and telling signs of potentially dangerous mental disturbance. It is hoped that a clear-headed understanding of serial killings can unlock better strategies to prevent, or even predict this rarest and most evil of crimes.